Samoyed Tales Trilogy

Celebrating Life, Love & Lessons with Our Dogs

By Jim Cheskawich,
Annie Reid, &
Cheryl Lynn West
with Celinda Cheskawich

Rex The Blizzard King Stories, LLC
December 2017
Woodland, Washington

Samoyed Tales Trilogy by Jim Cheskawich, Annie Reid, and Cheryl Lynn West with Celinda Cheskawich

Copyright © 2017 by Jim Cheskawich

All rights reserved. No portion of this book may be reproduced in any form without written permission from the publisher, except as permitted by U.S. copyright law. For permissions, contact the publisher at www.rexofwhiteway.com.

Although every precaution has been taken to verify the accuracy of the information contained herein, the authors and publisher assume no responsibility for any errors or omissions. No liability is assumed for damages that may result from the use of information contained within.

Published by Rex the Blizzard King Stories, LLC in Woodland, Washington. www.rexofwhiteway.com

ISBN: 978-0-9883640-6-6

Developmental Editing and Design: Lynne Holsapple

Text Editing and Proofing: Jim Cheskawich, Annie Reid, Cheryl Lynn West

Book Layout, Formatting, and Design: Lynne Holsapple and Kristie Kempker, Visually Speaking

Front Cover: Photo by Beth Ortensi, used with permission.

With deep appreciation to the Rex of White Way Samoyed Memorial Library and Museum for pictures of Rex of White Way and other Samoyeds from the Jim and Marian Osborn, Walt and Jan Kauzlarich, and Madelin Druse Collections. And also appreciation to Celinda Cheskawich, Heather Kelly, Mardee Ward-Fanning, Anne O'Neill, Joan Luna Liebes, Linda Martinson, and Cynthia Fleenor for the use of their photos.

To contact the authors:

Jim Cheskawich - www.rexofwhiteway.com; samtres@earthlink.net

Annie Reid - www.byanngharaad.com; annie.reid@cox.net

Cheryl Lynn West - CastleSamoyeds@earthlink.net; https://cheryllynnwest.com/

This collection of stories from different authors celebrates the Samoyed dog and captures the special bond between man and this ancient breed. We hope that you enjoy each story and know that you will understand the Samoyed dog better after joining us in this exploration of improbable and fascinating tales.

We thank Lynne Holsapple for being our editor, Kristie Kempker for formatting for Kindle, and our Samoyeds for serving as the inspiration for these anecdotal stories. A portion of the net proceeds of the book sales will go to The Rex of White Way Samoyed Memorial Library and Museum.

Table of Contents

Part I - Tales of Spirit Samoyeds and Other Spirited Dog Stories
    By Jim Cheskawich with Celinda Cheskawich

Introduction 9

Chapter 1 Rex of White Way 13

Chapter 2 Ono 43

Chapter 3 Riley 53

Chapter 4 Samantha Cotton Candy 69

Chapter 5 General and His Gift to Me 73

Chapter 6 Noah 79

Chapter 7 Seattle 81

Chapter 8 Cami Camillia 91

Chapter 9 Cricket 101

Chapter 10 Rebel 103

Chapter 11 Purple Girl 105

Chapter 12 Madelin Druse 107

Chapter 13 Honor 109

Chapter 14 Ending 111

Credits for Part I 114

Part II - Ever After
    By Annie Reid

Prologue - Niki: My Angel of Destiny 119

Beau: My Angel of Enlightenment 123

Cornelia: My Angel of Compassion 131

Tristan: The Angel of My Heart 141

Jamie: The Angel of All My Dreams Come True.................. 147

Geilie: My Angel of Pure Joy..................................... 161

Tributes and Disclaimers.. 173

Epilogue... 175

References and Sources... 176

Part III - Not Far From My Heart
    By Cheryl Lynn West

First in My Heart - Alicia....................................... 181

A New Friend - Ditty 191

My Sweet Baby Boy - Duncan................................... 197

About the Authors 204

Part I

Tales of Spirit Samoyeds
and
Other Spirited Dog Stories

By Jim Cheskawich with Celinda Cheskawich

Treasure Island 1938 with Agnes and Aljean Mason's White Way Samoyed Team. Courtesy of the Kauzlarich Collection.

Introduction

The Samoyed is surely a breed with many magical qualities. The book *Samoyeds*, written in 1934 by W. Lavallin Puxley, first captured for me some of the unusual antics and behaviors of these gentle creatures. Humorous and engaging stories of Samoyeds are presented; the book describes their encounters with hedgehogs, goldfish, geese, rats, and cats and their effect on humans.

Sometimes in our close relationships with dogs, we encounter phenomena without ready explanation that suggest another dimension beyond the accessibility of our five senses. While working on my first book, *The Story of Rex of White Way, The Blizzard King,* unusual events were reported to me by others and experienced firsthand during the research and interviews about Rex's life.

I was careful, however, not to use specifics in the Rex book as it might have served to diminish the believability of the biography. Similarly, with Ono and Riley who appear in the appendix to Rex's book, unexplainable occurrences became almost the norm after both died.

Even with the passage of time, some events cannot be explained or rationalized, and the mysteries remain puzzling. This short collection of stories in Part I is based on my firsthand observations and inferences from dog behavior that would be considered unusual and paranormal. Other canine behaviors described in this collection show the whimsical nature and thinking capability of the Samoyed, a multifaceted and charming breed.

I have lived with many Samoyeds either on my own or with my wife, Celinda, since 1991. I have also been the past president for the Samoyed Club of America (SCA) and served as its national treasurer for many years. I don't write or work in fiction because I like to look at just the facts or what appears to be the evidence at hand. My second book was an autobiographical account of my tour with the 101st Airborne Division during the Vietnam War. After recently reading Tim O'Brien's *The Things They Carried*, which reflected upon his own Vietnam War experience, I felt encouraged to take risks with my writing but still focus on what I know or think I know. Reading Beatrice Lydecker-Hayford's *Walking the Thin Veil* brought to mind my own experiences that were without explanation.

As background to this collection of stories, Samoyeds are a double-coated Arctic breed and were "discovered" when polar explorers in the latter half of the nineteenth century needed reliable means of transportation and used sled dogs to map and explore the North and South Poles. Samoyeds can be white, crème, biscuit, or any combination and are considered a medium-sized dog. When first found by European and Russian explorers, Samoyeds were also black and brown. Over time, black and brown were eliminated from official breed standards and breeding programs in England and the U.S.

Before acquiring my first Samoyed (Samantha), I read as much as I could about this northern breed. I remember the wording in various publications describing how the Samoyed was considered a "magical" breed, but I dismissed this as rhetorical hyperbole. Each Samoyed is unique, with no two alike, as with humans. They can be high maintenance, and not all "Sams" that I have observed exhibited unusual canine behavior—or maybe I just didn't watch them long enough. It is a smart breed although not considered the smartest when compared to the Poodle or Border Collie breeds. They do have an almost human like understanding, and that may be because of their long association with man.

Samoyeds are considered to be one of the oldest breeds, having evolved from the wolf. Research on evolution from the wolf to the dog suggests that evolution took place several times in history since the Ice Age ended about fifteen thousand to eighteen thousand years ago. It is also believed that evolution occurred in at least two or three distinct geographic locations, including points separated by thousands of miles in China and Europe.

The modern day Samoyed was considered by Jim Osborn—respected Samoyed historian, statistician, engineer, and researcher—to have existed possibly fifteen hundred years in its present form. After the Ice Age, dogs were used as hunters, guard dogs, partners, companions, herders, and draft animals, working closely with people and helping them in their rough life on the frozen tundra. The Samoyed people who dwelled west of the Ural Mountains in Siberia and north of the Arctic Circle are credited with domesticating the early dog into what we now know as the Samoyed.

The historical timeline shows a close association between canines and humans going back many thousands of years. The dog is considered the first domesticated animal. Even though cats are more popular than dogs in the U.S., the cat was a holdout and didn't become domesticated until three thousand to four thousand years ago. Archaeological findings from thousands of years ago in Asia indicate that dogs were sometimes buried with their owners so that they could guard the entrance to the afterlife, which was believed to face west. This was well before the European explorers visited America.

With this background on the Samoyed, the following is a collection of short stories describing the magical and oftentimes entertaining facets of these dogs' fascinating lives. These anecdotes have been recorded here so that someday we might have more complete explanations.

Agnes and Aljean Mason Samoyeds exhibited at L.A. Sportsman's Show with Rex of White Way as lead dog. Chief Betty Joe Houck on sled and Diana Dixon-Whistler. Circa early 1950's.

Chapter 1

Rex of White Way

Rex was a Samoyed who was bred by Agnes and Aljean Mason of White Way Kennels of Sacramento, California, and who lived from 1946 to 1957. He left his mark on breeding programs. Jim Osborn ranked Rex as the number one early American bred male in terms of his contribution to the current gene pool. Yet Rex never made AKC Champion as he missed a lot of show time while in his prime due to his rescue work. My way of thinking is that poor Rex had to compete often against Agnes' Ch. Silver Streak, and he couldn't beat that dog—yet Silver Streak was nowhere near Rex's equal out on the trail nor in his contribution to breeding programs. Rex is buried on Agnes Mason's old kennel property where she used to tell our mutual Rex friend, Kay Ketchum, that behind the house was "sacred ground," implying that Rex was buried there.

Rex had been dead for over forty-five years when I started researching his life. I was frustrated when I kept encountering roadblocks as I tried to locate Rex's former trainer, Lloyd Van Sickle, by searching internet obituaries for Lloyd and looking for contact information for his son, Steve, who had also worked with Rex and raced sled dogs. I had spent months keying into the search engines "Lloyd Van Sickle and Samoyeds."

One Sunday night during the winter of 2004, Celinda wanted to watch a movie on television that did not interest me. Out of boredom, I was back in the upstairs computer room that Celinda used for her SCA recording secretary job, and this time I typed into the search engine "Lloyd Van Sickle and Targhee Hounds." Within a few seconds on the old dial-up computer, entries appeared showing that Lloyd had been the topic of conversation within the past few months concerning the Targhee Hounds he was training. Nothing about Samoyeds or Rex of White Way appeared in the chat room topics, but it looked like Lloyd was still alive. But where was he living? I called Celinda away from her TV movie to tell her that finding recent information on Lloyd Van Sickle indicating he was alive was like finding Amelia Earhart still out in the Pacific Ocean hanging on to a propeller blade from her airplane.

I had a copy of a small, neatly trimmed picture of Rex of White Way from an old pedigree guide produced by the Trustees of the Goodrich Fund. I signed into the chat room quickly, asked for information on where I could find Lloyd Van Sickle, and placed the cut out picture of Rex of White Way on the keyboard. I told Rex to "Go find your master!" That was the start of delving into the real Rex, outside of reviewing old magazine articles Celinda had collected from primarily the *Western Kennel World* and the Bob and Dolly Ward book, *The New Complete Samoyed*. I needed firsthand accounts of the real Rex, and no one could be better than his trainer, Lloyd.

The next morning, there was an email response from a friend of Lloyd Van Sickle reporting that Lloyd had been at his house down by Mt. Shasta, California, just the previous night. Celinda kept me informed by telephone of this new development as I had gone to work early in the morning as a substitute teacher in one of the Battle Ground area schools. Celinda wrote back for us and obtained Lloyd's address and phone number in southern Oregon. When I returned home that night around 6:00 p.m., I quickly called Lloyd and told him of my interest in writing about Rex of White Way.

The project really began moving with a visit to Lloyd's place in southern Oregon and my newfound energy for gathering stories, newspaper and magazine articles, along with pictures of Rex of White Way. Most of the details on how the Rex story came together are laid out in the book, *The Story of Rex of White Way, The Blizzard King*. Two stories, though, are not in the book. One happened during the research interviews. The other event happened in January 2013 during the Rex book signing celebration at the Cottonwood Inn Restaurant in Truckee, California. The Cottonwood Inn had been named "Hilltop Lodge" during the time Rex and Lloyd lived in one of the five cabins nearby; it was renamed over a decade ago.

~ ~ ~

The first time Celinda and I visited the Cottonwood Inn/Hilltop Lodge was during the summer of 2005. We arrived early in the afternoon before the restaurant opened and befriended one of the gardening staff workers who asked us if we knew the place that we were about to enter was haunted. We tried to get more information from the female worker, but she was reticent about giving us any details. She advised us that we would have to find out for ourselves. Our curiosity was awakened, and we looked forward to discovering everything possible about the place so we could form our own conclusions.

We were soon greeted by the maître d', and we asked him why someone would tell us the place was haunted. He said he had no idea but had worked at the place for a number of years and never experienced anything unusual. We asked him if we could take a tour of the place before our dinner, and he motioned to go ahead, telling us to enjoy our visit. We turned to the left off the main entrance and crossed over to the central waiting area, which had several chairs, a brown leather lounge sofa, a few table lamps, and a fireplace with two small figurines carved into the marble frame at the top on both sides. It was dark inside, and the outside sun provided barely any light for the room.

As I recall, the off-white figurines had an almost grotesque expression that gave the impression of something sinister or otherworldly. We noticed very old sleds, skis, and ski equipment on the walls, as well as other antiques. Many framed pictures were displayed showing skiers, the Hilltop ski lift, and happy faces enjoying the outdoors; some photos dated back to the 1930s. Rex and Lloyd were conspicuously absent from the collection of pictures. It seemed odd to both Celinda and me.

Many decades ago, the Hilltop Lodge had been the site of the first mechanized ski lift west of the Mississippi River and had been used for Sierra Sled Club meetings. It had also served as an ad hoc "command central" when Rex and Lloyd lived in one of the cabins just a few yards away. This was the staging area when Rex, Lloyd, the Samoyeds, and the Targhee Hounds made their rescues. Their adventures had included rescuing planes downed at the Truckee airfield, delivering medical services to the stranded *"The City of San Francisco"* train stuck in a blizzard in twenty to thirty feet of snow up near Donner Pass, and traveling by sled team into remote cabin areas or houses in Truckee to rescue snowbound residents or seasonal lodgers.

We also learned in discussions with restaurant staff that at one time there were buildings on both sides of the Hilltop. The one closest to the main road and the first visible structure when approaching the Hilltop had burned down or been torn down. We went outside to investigate but couldn't make out what might have been there fifty-five to sixty-five years ago during Rex's reign. We were told this was a dormitory that had been in use for many years, but only a few red bricks remained. Celinda and I collected a few of the bricks and took them back in our car to our Woodland, Washington, home where they graced our lavender garden and also served as grave markers for our deceased Samoyeds.

The building on the other side of the Hilltop had once been a gambling, partying, drinking establishment. The stories we heard had violent themes of killings by gun or a knifing after the men got liquored up and dueled for the affections of the women working there. Celinda and I walked around the worn-down, greenish-brown building with loose wooden panels but thought it now seemed like more of a storage area for grounds maintenance. We did not sense any danger, the place's reputation, or anything unusual that might have happened or could occur there in the future.

We went back inside the Hilltop and were escorted to our table as early dinner was being served. We had arrived ahead of the usual evening crowd and could leisurely place our order. Just before dessert was ordered, Celinda had to use the restroom, and I saw my window of opportunity to get more information on the ghost appearances. I asked our waitress if she thought the place was haunted. She paused a second and responded, "Oh, yes!" I asked her what she could tell me as we wanted to know. I didn't tell her we were in town working on the Rex of White Way story, so what she had to say was shocking.

She said she had no personal stories, but one night about two years earlier, her waitress friend, who had since moved to the Midwest, had been working after 2:00 a.m. cleaning up the tables and chairs and putting the place back in order for the next work day. There were two people left to clean up: her waitress friend and the bartender. The bartender had collected change, beer bottles, cans, and glasses on his tray as he was almost finished closing up for the night. Then, back by the restroom area, he observed a white dog and an elderly white-haired hunched-over man walking aimlessly for a brief period and then going directly into the wall and disappearing. The bartender dropped his tray with the money, bottles, and glasses and ran with the waitress out to the cold parking lot and waited for about thirty minutes to calm down. He returned to quickly clean up the broken bottles and glasses, take the money from the cash register, grab coats, lock the front door, and get out!

Our waitress said that nothing else like that had ever happened that she was personally aware of, but she had heard other stories about unusual events that had typically taken place between the fireplace area and the restrooms. About this time Celinda returned and complained about the framed picture in the women's bathroom that just wouldn't hang level on the wall even though it looked like it used to or should. I then asked the waitress to repeat the story for Celinda.

After hearing the same story I heard, my ex-wife, Celinda surmised that I had prompted the waitress to tell the story for her amusement, and she asked how much of a tip I had promised for such a tall tale. The waitress said that whomever or whatever is back there knew we were coming because a mirror had fallen off the wall overnight in the women's bathroom, revealing a new hole in the wall. Because the mirror had broken, restaurant staff had replaced it with a small framed picture, trying for hours to get it to hang level like the mirror used to.

Then Celinda exchanged phone numbers with the waitress as she wanted contact information for her waitress friend who had moved to the Midwest. Over the following months, we were unable to corroborate the story further but did know that we needed to make another trip to the Hilltop soon.

Without further incident, Celinda and I left the restaurant for the evening, carefully picking up more of the very best red bricks from the demolished house next door to the Hilltop. We had to have something that Rex had seen or been near, and this was the best we thought we could do!

~ ~ ~

Several years passed, and we spent our time working on a movie about Rex, a U.S. postage stamp request for Rex, a plan for a six-episode TV series on Rex, and a seven-minute pilot video to serve as a marketing aid. The writer-editor (Vicki Weiland) for the pilot video encouraged me to begin writing the book. We finished the book first as everything was ready with the storyline, pictures, and personal recollections from those who knew Rex, Lloyd, or Agnes Mason. The Gertrude Adams' files (that were part of the Jim and Marian Osborn Collection) contained references to doing a movie about Rex as early as the 1950s. Adams believed there was enough material to even do a book on Agnes Mason based on her contributions to California politics and lifestyle; her Samoyed dog breeding, showing, sledding, and club activities; as well as her work activities and businesses.

The Rex book came together magically with photographs and permissions arriving just in time for production. Otherwise, we were prepared to go to press without certain pictures. An unknown force always seemed to be driving the book's completion as it never seemed like work to me. I did imagine many times that Rex should be pretty pleased with himself—wherever he was. Just days before we were set to go to press, Rex's puppy picture (and others that were used in the book) arrived in the mail from Kay Ketchum.

After *The Story of Rex of White Way, The Blizzard King* was published in November 2012, we quickly planned on a book signing/book completion party up at the Hilltop if we could find a break in the snow season for just a few days. The date was set for mid-January 2013 to coincide with the sixty-one year anniversary of Rex's delivery of Dr. Nelson and medical supplies to the passengers and crew aboard the snowbound *City of San Francisco* stuck up at Yuba Gap near Donner Pass. We invited one of the skiers who was brought in from Reno, Nevada, to deliver food supplies on skis to the people stranded on the train back in 1952. The gentleman, now close to eighty years old, told us how the snow had come down sideways so that he couldn't see more than a few feet in front of himself as he and another skier took some food in small bags for the hungry passengers and train crew. We marveled at how Rex could have led the team over the mountain ridge, probably, to descend down to the train as that appeared to be the only approach.

About twenty-five to thirty people attended, including my editor Vicki Weiland, my book designer Desta Garrett, Kay Ketchum, Celinda and her partner Russ, and other friends and invited guests. I also met Gayleen Hays, the author of *Policewoman One: My 20 Years on the LAPD*, and want to give her credit and thank her for inspiring me to write my own memoirs of my service time in Vietnam.

As the evening progressed, one of the guests—another author—rose to give a speech and to toast Rex with his champagne-filled glass. At the moment he said, "This is to Rex," his crystal glass shattered in his hand. The author said he wasn't cut and that Rex or Rex's spirit caused the glass to shatter at the instant when Rex's name was mentioned. He carefully wrapped up the glass shards in his white dinner napkin and placed it in his coat pocket as a reminder of the evening and the power of Rex. I filmed his toast to Rex on my camera but was partially blocked, so I couldn't catch how the glass actually shattered in his hand.

We thereafter commenced with interviewing the skier from sixty-one years earlier as he sat by the logs flickering in the fireplace. We recorded the interview on film using a tripod borrowed from the restaurant. I was watching closely for anything unusual as were Russ, Celinda, Vicki, and Kay. I had to use the restroom at one point and instructed Celinda and Russ to come get me if I didn't return in a minute to the main group. After I returned, I asked Celinda to check the status of the mirror in the women's restroom and look for a hole in the wall as we had been through this routine once before a few years earlier. Celinda reported that nothing out of the ordinary was going on.

As we were about to wrap up the evening and head back to our hotel rooms in Truckee, Celinda and I struck up a conversation with one of the restaurant staff workers who had worked there for a few years. He did not want to be identified, but he told us a story. Several years ago he was in the back area one early afternoon in the restaurant before opening time. He noticed a very old man dressed in dark work clothes from another era with a pocket watch. The man was hunched over, thin, had white hair, and said nothing. With him was a white dog. The worker asked how he had gotten into the closed restaurant and what he was doing here, but the man and the dog then turned away without a word and disappeared into the wall. The man was visibly upset and shaking when he told us this story, but I promised I would never use his name.

Back at home after the successful book signing and celebratory party, I had phone conversations with Kay Ketchum, Alta Van Sickle (Lloyd's widow), and Steve Van Sickle (Lloyd's son). The belief among the three was that it was "Uncle Lou" who was disappearing into the walls up at the Hilltop. Decades ago, he was cared for and looked after by Lloyd Van Sickle. Uncle Lou pretty much walked around the Hilltop wherever he pleased, and he liked to have a Samoyed with him. I don't recall being told he had a specific job, but Lou helped Lloyd sometimes in completing a task. As for the white dog, I don't think it was small like a Bichon. Lloyd wouldn't have any use for a dog that couldn't work for his meals. There are only a few breeds with white coats. Was it Rex? Rex used to run around loose up at the Hilltop while the other White Way Samoyeds were staked out. How can I prove or disprove it?

Rex was just an uncommon Samoyed who saved human lives for a living, followed the static in the telephone lines once to get home in a blizzard with the sled team, had a world record in weight pulling, followed his canine instincts, played the piano, sang, and is an ancestor of almost every Samoyed in the U.S. today except for those few recently imported into the country. Hopefully someday we will find out concrete answers—I have recorded it here for future generations to unravel. When Agnes Mason said Rex could do just about anything, and Lloyd Van Sickle confirmed for me that Rex would do anything he asked him to do, including climbing a tree, they couldn't envision Rex hanging around for seventy years in one form or another.

Rex still knows how to win—even in the publishing field. If he is still hanging around, I hope he enjoyed his own book and his Rex of White Way Samoyed Memorial Library and Museum, which was approved by the IRS as a not-for-profit 501(c)(3) organization on the first attempt and within seven weeks of submission. I don't think it can be done any faster, so this was an unexpected surprise.

Rex started off in 2013 by winning gold, silver, and bronze eBook and eLit awards in the category of Nonfiction Animal and Pet books. In February 2014, he won the Maxwell Award from the Dog Writers Association of America as the Best Single Breed book for 2013. In 2015 Rex's book hit number one on Amazon Free Kindle downloads in the category of Children's Nonfiction Animal Books. During Thanksgiving Week of that year, Rex had over five hundred free downloads. He started off the week around number nine, rose to number two after a few days, and on Black Friday, November 27, 2015, he finished the five-day "race" at number one for several hours as the day came to a close. He wasn't going to lose. Lloyd Van Sickle was once told at the start of a speed race that he wasn't going to win anything with that white dog, but Rex still knows how to finish. He ran up the rankings again on July 10, 2016, making it to number two in the category of free Amazon Kindle, Children's Nonfiction Animal books.

When *The Story of Rex of White Way* went to press, reports on Rex's height had him somewhere between twenty-four and twenty-seven inches at the withers. As Mel Fishback once wrote in an article for *Organization for the Working Samoyed (OWS)*, stories about Rex became exaggerated and embellished over time—including his height. However, with the establishment of the Rex of White Way Samoyed Memorial Library and Museum, materials were donated to the Library, including the Jim and Marian Osborn Collection, which included measurements taken of Rex for the *Illustrated Standard* project. Rex's measurements are neatly handwritten (most probably by Gertrude Adams) in a column under his name:

Overall Length	24 ½"
Shoulder Height	24"
Hip Height	24"
Shoulder Width	7 5/8"
Hip Width	7 5/8"
Elbow Height	13 ¼"
Hock Height	7"
Tail Height	8 ¾"
Chest Depth	10 ¼"
Rib Spring	7 ¼"
Rib Girth	28 ½"
Head Overall	9 1/8"
Muzzle Length	3 ¾"
Muzzle Girth	12"
Width between Eyes	2 ¼"
Width between Ears	4 ½"
Ear to Eye	4"
Ear Length	4"
Waist	18"

Of the three dozen dogs and bitches charted, no one else had a waist as small as Rex. In typical English understatement, as was said about the immortal English Champion, Kara Sea, Rex was "quite a good dog."

*Mason Team with Rex of White Way in lead at Donner Summit.
On left (near side) behind Rex in order: Toby, Czar, Jacko, Trooper.
On right (far side) behind Rex are Ted (sold to Constable Johnson), Jumbo, Homer, Tim.
Circa late 1940's or early 1950's. Courtesy of the Kauzlarich Collection.*

Rex at lead with Lloyd Van Sickle on sled-1950. Toby, Tim, and Homer behind Rex on near side with Ted, Junker, and Jack behind Rex on far side. Courtesy of the Kauzlarich Collection.

Mason Samoyeds and Targhee Hounds delivering mail in Idaho in a blizzard. Lloyd Van Sickle-Driver. Courtesy of the Kauzlarich Collection.

*Agnes Mason proudly holding Rex of White Way and Toby the Malamute after they both broke world weight pulling records on the same day.
Courtesy of the Kauzlarich Collection.*

*Samoyed and Targhee Teams (17 in all) in training by Lloyd Van Sickle for American Dog Derby Races by carrying the mail between Drummond and Squirrel.
Photo courtesy of the Kauzlarich Collection.*

Rex of White Way of Truckee, California sets a world record as a 7 year old Samoyed owned by Mr. and Mrs. A.E. Mason. Rex weighed 70 pounds and pulled 1,870 pounds at a meet in West Yellowstone, Montana on February 22, 1954. Courtesy of the Kauzlarich Collection.

*Race with Lloyd Van Sickle and Rex of White Way the Lead Dog.
Courtesy of the Kauzlarich Collection.*

Lloyd Van Sickle with Rex at Lead. Courtesy of the Kauzlarich Collection.

Mason's Samoyeds and Targhees pulling out a plane that was forced down in 1949 by Truckee California Airfield. Courtesy of Kauzlarich Collection.

Rex, Lloyd, and the Targhees making the mail run. Courtesy of the Kauzlarich Collection.

This is a post card with "Mason Samoyede Kennels, Mr. and Mrs. A. E. Mason, Rt.7, Box 3483, Sacramento, CA" on the back. Rex is at lead.
Courtesy of the Kauzlarich Collection.

This is the Mason Team ready to deliver the mail after off load from a plane. Back of post card reads: "Mason's famous Samoyed Dog. Rex-lead dog noted for being able to face blizzards and cross-country travel. This team was entered in the Sierra Dog Derby Races March 5th and 6th at Truckee, CA."
Courtesy of the Kauzlarich Collection.

Rex and Lloyd going over race strategy. Courtesy Mardee Ward-Fanning.

Samoyed Team used to promote the Inaugural Polar Route departing from San Francisco Airport. Probably the White Way Team with Rex. Courtesy Anne O'Neill.

Rex's Sons: Winter Trail Blizzard (L) and Ch. Winter Trail Blazer (R) at the National Specialty L.A. Show 1955. Owned by Mr. and Mrs. Charles Burr. Courtesy of Osborn Collection.

Ch. Winter Trail Blazer 10-57. Sire-Rex of White Way and Dam-Chastuska of Encino, CDX. Courtesy of Osborn Collection.

Winter Trail Silver Trinket (Rex daughter) 5/60. Courtesy of Osborn Collection.

Ch. Tarko's Kazan of Encino (Kazan) filling in for Rex while he was probably out working; Rex's offspring: Trinket (B), Blitz, Blazer, Rogue (Males); Chastuska of Encino (Tussy) 12/53. Courtesy of Osborn Collection.

Winter Trails Rogue was first in American Bred with 13 in class at the National Specialty Show, L.A. Kennel Club-1955. Courtesy Osborn Collection.

World record holder-Rex of White Way. Picture taken right after he set the record as strongest dog in the world. This is the "keyboard" picture and the one shown to Riley before his National Best in Show win. Courtesy Mardee Ward-Fanning.

Mason Team with Rex at lead and Lloyd Van Sickle the driver. Courtesy Osborn Collection.

Twenty five dog team with lead-Rex of W.W. at San Mateo, CA. SCA National Specialty in August 1952 held at Bay Meadows. Rex was magnificent leading this team driven by noted musher and trainer of Mason Teams-Lloyd Van Sickle. They went the mile of the track in a beautiful gallop and not a growl in the crowd and yet each team had never seen the other teams until that moment. Courtesy Osborn Collection.

ASHTON IDAHO 1946
LEAD CH NICK OF WHITEWAY
2ND RIGHT CH WHITEWAY OF KOBE
2ND LEFT CH HERDSMAN'S CHATTIGAN
3RD RIGHT CH BOREAUS OF FARSTEMES
3RD LEFT CH STARCHAK CD

Mason Samoyeds parachuted in Idaho with Ch. Petrof's Nick-leader. Circa 1948. Courtesy Osborn Collection.

An airborne White Way Samoyed. Courtesy Osborn Collection.

33

Rex, the White Way Samoyed Team, Lloyd and Alta Van Sickle breaking trail. Courtesy the Kauzlarich Collection.

Rex in lead with Lloyd and Alta Van Sickle on the sled. Alta was sure Rex couldn't hear any commands barked out by Lloyd with the roar of the falls below. But Rex knew what to do. Courtesy Kauzlarich Collection

Rex and Lloyd—with mutual trust they bonded forever.
Courtesy Kauzlarich Collection.

Rex and Aljean Mason in the Conformation Ring where he was W.D. and B.O. in 1951.
Courtesy Kauzlarich Collection.

Lloyd and Rex. Courtesy Kauzlarich Collection.

White Way Samoyeds at the show-left to right: Jacko, Ch. Silver Streak, Ch. Nick, and Romeo. Rex had to go up against Silver Streak in the ring but Rex had no equal out in the snow. Courtesy Kauzlarich Collection.

*The White Way Team With Mayor Rossi of S.F. in 1938.
Courtesy Kauzlarich Collection.*

Mason Samoyed Dog Team, Aljean Mason, Driver

*A Young Aljean Mason Driving the Mason Sled Team-Circa Mid to Late 1930's.
Courtesy Kauzlarich Collection.*

*Rex of White Way Head Study with Alta Van Sickle.
Courtesy Kauzlarich Collection*

Rex-Lead Dog with Mason's Famous Samoyed Team exhibited at California State Fair 1948. Lloyd Van Sickle the driver and Lou Hawkes and Jenny Gracia-passengers. Courtesy Kauzlarich Collection.

Rex and the team tuning up at the 1948 California State Fair. Lloyd the driver with Lou Hawkes and Jenny Gracia as passengers. Courtesy Kauzlarich Collection.

L.A. Sportsman's Show, Circa Early 1950's, with Rex and the White Way Samoyed Team. Courtesy Kauzlarich Collection.

Rex at lead delivering the U.S. Mail with Targhee Hounds and White Way Samoyeds behind him. Rex sometimes led two mail runs of different teams on the same day and so he was allowed a "cat nap." Courtesy Kauzlarich Collection.

Lloyd was mocked ahead of the speed race that he couldn't win anything with that white dog. But here is Rex in the Winner's Circle with a proud Lloyd and the Targhee Hound Speed Team. West Yellowstone, Montana February 22, 1953.
Courtesy Kauzlarich Collection.

Rex at lead with Mason Samoyed Team and Lloyd Van Sickle the Driver at a Ski Cabin. Behind Rex on the near side of Rex-Toby, Czar, Jacko, and Ch. Trooperine. On the far side of Rex to his rear-Ted, Jumbo, "Unidentified" (by Agnes Mason on picture back), and Tim. Courtesy Kauzlarich Collection.

Chapter 2

Ono

Multi-BISS CH. Oakbrooks Strike It Rich, also known as Ono, was considered by some as THE dog of his generation. He finished 2001 as the number one Samoyed male and was the number one Samoyed in the country until the 2001 SCA National Show when he was awarded Best of Opposite Sex. Ono and his owners, Alan and Jane Stevenson, skipped the December 2001 Northeast shows since he had never flown at that point. He needed a few more Breed points to move back into the number one Samoyed spot, but the Stevensons didn't want to put him on a plane.

I remember competing with Alan Stevenson for the first time in the ring in Frederick, Maryland, at the 2000 SCA National. I was showing a puppy male out of Seattle's first litter, and Alan also had a puppy in the six to nine month class from his Oakbrook line. I remember clearly thinking that here was a guy I could beat as his puppy was rolling on the floor, and it looked like Alan could have cared less. Wearing his green jacket and pumpkin orange tie, he was often down on the floor with the puppy. As I recall, neither of us received a ribbon in that class. A few days later at the end of the week, Alan was in the ring again with a smooth floating Samoyed who stood out from the crowd for the almost seven hours of Best of Breed judging.

That Samoyed was named Ono, and the team of Alan and Ono won the 2000 SCA National Show with Best of Breed. I kept wondering how this guy could learn so much in just four days, but he did have Ono. He told me later that his theory was to get the dog to relax when a puppy so that he or she would learn to enjoy and wait with anticipation for the ring and show time. Ono was a seasoned professional, and Alan handled him differently than the puppy. He expected and asked for more—and Ono delivered. But Alan's daughter, Heather, told me later that Alan used to get down on the floor even with Ono at his winning National as the wait was so long. She said in the year that Ono won the National, she saw a picture taken of Ono asleep in the ring right before he won that show.

As SCA president, I was supposed to be in the show win picture with the judge, Alan, and Ono, but I missed that as I was back in the hotel room changing. I caught up just as the picture session was finished with Ono.

At the SCA Awards ceremony on Saturday night, a few hours after Best of Breed judging had concluded, I broke precedent as SCA president by asking Alan to come up to the podium and tell us what it was like to win a National. I think Jane found him celebrating his win in the bar where he probably had something stronger than a cola in his glass. That was my introduction to the team of Alan, Jane, and Ono. Celinda had met Ono as a puppy at the Washington State Samoyed Specialty show when Ono and our Cricket visited the show ring before anyone else was there.

Celinda bred Cricket with Ono shortly after that Specialty, and quickly developed a strong friendship. My wife and I prevailed on Alan and Jane Stevenson to join us with Ono by flying to the first ever AKC-Eukanuba Classic in Orlando, Florida, in December of 2001. As a result, I got to stay with Ono for a few days and walk him in the mornings, take him for rides in our Ford Cargo Van for coffee and the newspaper, and just hang out with Alan and Ono at the time-share, which was a wedding present from my sister to Celinda and me. Since this was just a few months after the September 11, 2001, terrorist attacks, the time-share was almost empty. I remember counting only thirteen residents out of maybe a possible 250 that would normally be in that Kissimmee, Florida, time-share. We had more grey squirrels in the parking lot than people staying there.

Ono slept each night in a crate on the driver's side in the back of the white Ford Cargo Van, which was parked behind the building away from the street lights and main entrance into the time-share. There was a large lake nearby, and Ono was entertained each night by the sound of frogs, ducks, and other native wildlife. I even took Ono to the Old Town part of Kissimmee one early morning where signs were posted saying "No Dogs," but I never considered that the ordinance applied to Ono because he was different. We enjoyed our walks along the stone paths with palm trees, large flowering plants, insects, floating butterflies, and carefully trimmed flower beds on the time-share property in the Florida sunshine. Sometimes a squirrel would dart in front of us. Ono saved his energy for more important things that were on his mind.

The day came for the big show at this first AKC-Eukanuba Classic, and Ono received an Award of Merit and won Best Bred by Exhibitor. We were very disappointed as we had expected Best of Breed and maybe a Group placement. It wasn't his best performance, and Ono seemed to be off his game just a little. Afterwards, when it was dark, I tried to feed Ono from the back of my van with moistened kibble on a plastic spoon, but he just spit the kibble about fifteen feet away in the direction of an Akita champion. I didn't want anyone to see Ono this way, so I stopped quickly. I wondered what the Akita thought of all this. Ono probably set the record that night for distance in expelling dog food.

The day of the flight back to California arrived, and we lent the Stevensons one of our crates in which to take Ono home as on the trip over they had realized a bigger crate was needed. On the green tape fastened to the crate, there was lettering, "Dog Inside," with a large black arrow pointing up. Celinda and I wished everyone a good journey and returned back to the time-share.

At the airport Alan had given me a picture of himself and Ono, and I remember taking it from my wallet when back at the time-share. I walked out the sliding glass door onto the balcony that overlooked the lake. I saw a strange series of air bubbles moving across the lake from the right to the left and watched the pattern for a few seconds. Then it disappeared. I looked down at the picture that I had held in my hand the entire time on the balcony. I had a feeling of something I was certain of but didn't know how or why I could know. I went back in the living room and approached Celinda with the picture. Pushing the picture into her hands, I said to Celinda that we would never see Alan again as he was going to die soon. I said to Celinda that a message of imminent death was in the picture, and whatever was going on in the lake with the air bubbles just confirmed it.

Celinda and I went into town to do some sightseeing for the rest of the afternoon, and we talked no more about the picture. That night we picked out a very nice restaurant from the travel guide, and the drive took us past Disney World. The evening seemed to be very peaceful with the early December setting sun, warm air, and almost no traffic. On our short trip from the time-share, we could see all the rides and the large swans that identified the Disney property. Celinda brought along her cell phone and made several attempts to receive incoming calls from our friend Christie Smith, but the calls always broke up before too long. We kept asking ourselves, "Why is Christie calling us so much?"

Once we were seated, Celinda finally had a good connection on her cell phone. Before we could even place our order, Celinda started crying and said Christie had tried to call her six times in the last half hour with some very bad news. Ono had suffered a horrific death on the return flight to LAX. The airline had put him in a non-pressurized part of the plane, causing his eardrum to burst before he froze to death on the flight home.

~ ~ ~

An hour after the plane landed at LAX in California, the Stevensons learned of Ono's death. Usually the dogs come out first and then the baggage. This time the order was reversed, and the handlers were nervous. The airport personnel finally opened the partition and started bringing out the dogs.

There were only five crates, and then they shut the door. Jane Stevenson frantically asked, "Where the h#$% is our dog? "The reply was, "Oh, he didn't make it." She asked, "What the h#$% do you mean by that? "The response was, "Oh, he died." That is how Alan and Jane found out that Ono was gone.

After considerable time had passed, Alan and Jane were allowed down the tarmac to see Ono, conveniently after the plane had already taken off to its next destination. What they saw was a smashed up crate in two pieces sitting beside their dead dog on the tarmac conveyor belt. The water, shaped like the water bowl, was found still frozen solid to Ono's neck fur—even two hours after landing.

The airline said they would do an autopsy to which Alan replied, "Over my dead body." Because of the rules and regulations, it was the airlines or airport veterinarian that had to do the autopsy. The Stevenson's veterinarian, after being awakened at 1:00 a.m., made the drive to LAX to observe the necropsy in which they learned that Ono had been in an uncontrolled area with pressure that had blown out his eardrum. He had then frozen to death in temperatures as low as seventy degrees below zero.

We learned later that the Stevensons had heard Ono frantically barking after take-off in Orlando. They had watched him being loaded onto the plane before their flight back and had told the pilot that a dog was onboard as did the other handlers who were on the flight. There were six dogs on that flight from the show.

I blamed myself for inviting the Stevensons even though they had not wanted to fly Ono. I had persisted and even lent them my crate for the return flight. A few days earlier Alan had given me the chance to keep Ono a little longer down in Orlando for other shows. I could have possibly taken him back up to Virginia for new shows and returned him to California later in January. But I wasn't a good enough handler and had said "No." Alan would have let me keep him a little longer.

~ ~ ~

Back at the restaurant table, neither Celinda nor I had much interest in our meal. I don't remember Celinda eating anything, and we probably took a "doggie bag" back to the time-share. We did toast Ono's life and all of our memories of this great dog. We talked about his importance to the breed with his offspring and his show wins and rankings. He was only four years old when he died, and his birthday was the day before his death. I reminded Celinda of the picture Alan had given me, the ripples on the water, and how it was an impending death (but not Alan's) that I foresaw.

That night through many tears, Celinda and I tried to get some sleep, any sleep. At one point after hours of tossing around, I felt a pressure on my left shoulder and knew it was Ono. He didn't say anything such as with a bark or whimper. I didn't think my heart could survive reaching around and feeling fur, pads, and toenails. I accepted this as Ono and didn't need to test it. He was still around, somewhere. I then fell asleep.

The next day was a show day as we had brought Mia (Ch. d'Keta's Go l'Diva, CGC, HCT-s) who was an Ono daughter. If I remember correctly, Mia earned two points at the show. She had her dad's movement but was only nine months old. After the show, we returned to the time-share and packed up to make the long trip back to Virginia. We didn't feel much like doing anything as we grieved. On the way out of the time-share, about a dozen squirrels appeared in the parking lot. Even they looked sad as they had been there when Ono was at the time-share; they were privileged to have seen a giant of a star in the Samoyed breed.

Celinda and I drove a little out of the way to reach the Atlantic so we could drop rose petals in the ocean in memory of Ono. On the drive back, I jotted down notes of my recollections of Ono on a napkin. I didn't see myself as a writer yet, so I wasn't sure what I would do with the scribbling I made while driving. It was a very quiet and solemn ride for both of us. On our return trip, we picked up all of our Samoyeds from Cheryl West in Cassleberry, Florida, as she had graciously watched most of our clan while we went on to Orlando to stay with Ono and the Stevensons. Now Ono was gone. I worried about the Stevensons and the Wards who co-owned Ono. I thought about the huge loss to the breed.

Back in Virginia, I took my camera film of Ono at the airport to a camera store in a mall in Rossyln, which was a few blocks away from my place of work. I needed to send the developed pictures showing the "Dog Inside" crate labeling to the Stevensons so that they could work out a settlement resolution with the airline carrier. Film usually took forty-eight hours to develop, but for some strange reason—and I began to call it the curse of Ono—the pictures didn't come out until the third attempt at processing. It took nearly two weeks to receive the pictures, which I quickly mailed on to the Stevensons.

Also at this time, I started typing a short article that I entitled "I Remember Ono." This, too, presented problems as my typed work got "lost" in the computer several times. I transferred the short story to a disc that quickly became corrupted. Eventually, I was able to type up three or four pages and save it for later use.

~ ~ ~

One Saturday a few months after Ono's passing, Celinda was stuffing envelopes for her recording secretary mailings and had several adults in the house helping her. When I returned home after working a half day at the office, an Ono son and an Ono daughter (our Mia) were breeding, and none of the adults present had noticed Mia was in season. This was clearly something that wasn't planned as Mia was barely a year old, and the breeding to her half-brother was too close. We wouldn't know for a month that she was pregnant, but I quickly drove her down to the Manassas, Virginia, veterinarian for a checkup as they were the only office within seventy-five miles still open late on a Saturday afternoon. My wife and I talked about the "Ono Curse" not being over yet. We were upset about the "oops breeding," and if I hadn't gone into work, maybe I would have been the one in the backyard watching the dogs—instead of several children present. I was the one who checked on the dogs in the backyard when I got back from work and found them breeding. There was nothing we could do about this but wait for nature to take its course.

After a month, Mia was retested, and she was definitely pregnant. About this time, I decided to take the early retirement offer at work, and we bought a house and kennel property in Woodland, Washington. We drove all six of our Sams across country, including Mia. As soon as we unpacked, Mia delivered six healthy puppies. However, Mia hadn't built up immunity long enough and around the tenth day, all of the puppies got sick with the herpes virus. We saved two after several thousand dollars in veterinarian bills, but these last two were not thriving as well as they should have been and were put down. They are buried in the lavender garden out in front of the kennel, and we named them "Ducky and The Beav" for the mascots of the University of Oregon (UO) and Oregon State University (OSU). We knew this was Ono's revenge. Mia went on to a short show career and was very competitive, earning her championship easily. She was placed with a junior handler who had her own successful career, but Mia died unexpectedly at seven years of age due to cancer.

About the time Mia found a good home with the junior handler, her brother, Riley, was returned to us. Riley gets his own chapter in this book. I thought Ono might even be overdoing his revenge bit for his horrible death on the plane when Riley came back home. No single Samoyed could ever be that bad—or could it?

~ ~ ~

The Stevensons will never fly a dog again, and Ono's flight to and from Orlando was the only flight they ever made with a dog. The day after Ono died, Alan and his daughter, Heather, had to go to the Long Beach, California, shows to hold the major. After the nightmare with Ono's death and only a couple hours of sleep, they drove together early in the morning to Long Beach, as Alan didn't want Heather to go to the show alone. When they arrived at the building for the show, everyone knew what had happened to Ono the day before and surrounded them. Sunshine, Ono's daughter, finished her championship that day. When the judge pointed to Sunshine and Heather, everyone started crying, and the judge looked confused and said, "Usually when I point for the win, everyone is happy. Why is everyone crying?"

Ono's entries for the Long Beach shows were cancelled that day. With Alan handling, Riley also got his first major the day after Sunshine finished. Heather didn't want her dad to walk away from Conformation dog shows. Alan showed Riley after that. Riley was the last dog Alan showed in Conformation unless Heather was overloaded with dogs, and Alan helped as a backup. Alan and Jane moved on to Agility events and never looked back to Conformation dog shows.

Anytime I hear "Pavane for a Dead Princess" by Maurice Ravel on a classical music station, I am reminded of Ono's greatness, very short life with a sad ending, and unfinished potential. I remember listening to the composition on the car radio the weekend of August 31, 1997, as the world mourned the passing of Princess Diana. I had been returning to Virginia on the five hour drive back from a Pennsylvania dog show after Rebel's five point major. Ravel seems to capture a deep sense of longing for another time on the world's stage in his "Pavane."

Even today, I can almost will Ravel's composition to play on Oregon's 89.9 FM radio station if I think of Ono for long. After Ono's death, I heard the piece quite frequently for several years and it seemed to capture an inordinate amount of airplay for a long time.

*Ono with Alan Stevenson, Judge Jeanne Nonhof, and Show Chair Charles Hurry after winning Best of Breed at the 2000 SCA National Specialty.
Photo courtesy Heather Kelly.*

Ono in his last picture ever taken at the Orlando Airport with Jane and Alan Stevenson and Celinda. Photo from Author's Collection.

Heather Kelly with Riley who is half asleep, the Author, Alan with Ono, Christie Smith, and Celinda with Mia at the 2001 SCA National Specialty. Riley wasn't going to put any effort into it unless it really counted. Courtesy Celinda Cheskawich.

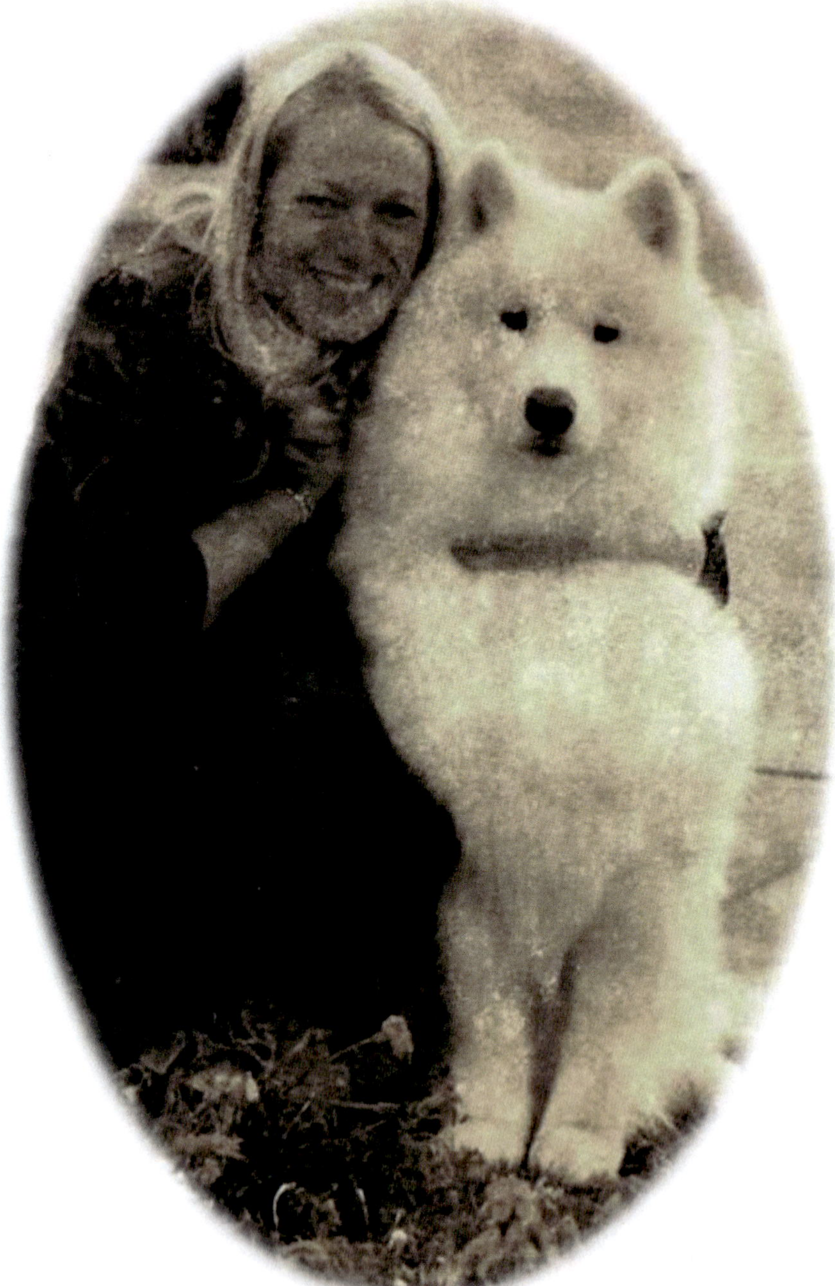

Chapter 3

Riley

Multi-BISS Ch. d'Keta Strikes Gold, HCT-s or "Riley" was out of Ch. Sanorka's Trip Into Tamara (Cricket) and Ono. Cricket was in labor but just couldn't deliver the puppies naturally; she had been digging a hole for a few days in the backyard and needed medical attention. For four days after the C-section, Cricket was observed outside on her breaks from nursing still digging at that hole. (A year earlier, I had seen Seattle deliver six puppies in sixty minutes for Celinda's and my first litter together, and I had thought that was the way it would always be. Christie Smith said we were just lucky with Seattle's first litter, and usually there are problems. Delivery isn't textbook perfect.)

This was Cricket's first litter. Celinda used a uterine contraction heart monitor but took her in with my Malamute owner friend, Denise, to the veterinarian's office in Manassas, Virginia, for a C-section around 10:00 p.m. on March 17, 2001. I went to bed early as I had my day job in Washington, DC, and needed to be in the office by 7:30 a.m. Celinda came home well after midnight with six puppies and Cricket. As Celinda told me the next day, "Green Boy" (a temporary name based on the color of ribbon or string used to tell the puppies apart) was blocked in one of the horns inside Cricket. The other five puppies were all together on the other side in the other horn. It appears that "Green Boy" (later named Riley) had already been singled out by nature for some reason. He always acted special.

Around 5:30 a.m. the next day, Celinda tried to get Cricket to nurse but "Cricky" was still too drugged up from the anesthesia. I got into the whelping box, picked up Cricket, and put her on her side like I did for grooming nails so she could nurse. Then we hooked up the six puppies for their first time. After a few days, it was pretty clear to me that one guy was the leader: Green Boy was the star singer and primary force. Nature had already "preselected" him as special.

He also started up a humming tune that was seven notes long and was repeated in an unbroken round by the whole group every time they nursed. I don't remember Cricket singing with them. Once they got the kibble, we took Cricket away so she wouldn't be too pushy around the food. Moistened kibble was served in a large pan with a raised centerpiece so a pup couldn't cross over and swim in the pan. Riley probably looked at it as a suitable challenge.

While eating, Green Boy/Riley would push everyone clockwise and then decide to stop, reverse, and push the whole group of puppies counterclockwise. All this was while they were lined up at the large pan in a circle eating and making a mess on their fronts. Riley grew long legs, and when the time came to place the puppies, I thought his legs were too long, and he was too thin. I couldn't wait to get this budding "bark star" on the plane and across the country to his new home on the West Coast. He went to live with the Stevensons in California. I never thought he would amount to anything and didn't even think "AKC Champion." I was sure he was just trouble. He was pushy.

As the months went on, Riley started his show career and picked up a few points (maybe pointers too) going to shows with his dad, Ono. I can imagine his sire telling him to save his best for last. Just barely seven months old, Riley won Best Puppy at the 2001 SCA National Show in Denver under Houston Clark. His sire won Best of Opposite Sex at the same show, his last SCA National. Riley continued his show career in California, sometimes acting like a show dog and most other times being disinterested in the ring.

Riley got bored easily and knew what to do with any free time. According to Alan, Riley's favorite pastime was chasing a tennis ball for as long as Alan's arm could throw the ball or hit it with a tennis racket. A close second in entertainment value for Riley was skating in the kitchen. He would gather up food and water pans and slide across the slick kitchen floor with his feet in the pans, hitting the walls, chairs, refrigerator, and oven, thereby making his own music. He tore up mattresses and sofas if left alone in the house, and I think he took out a lot of plaster from walls. We heard stories that Riley would go in the front end of a restaurant or pizza place in California and find his way out the back door, quickly sending everyone in pursuit. As soon as young Riley got his AKC Conformation Championship, he was brought up to Oregon because I think he had grown too big for his britches.

The moment we reconnected with Riley at Christie's place in Portland, Oregon, he spotted a squirrel as soon as he saw us and got away to entertain himself. (I was told he won't run off lead, so chill out Jim as he always listens.) I wasn't surprised he chased after the squirrel, and he covered almost half the small neighborhood before we corralled him. He ended up in one home for a couple of weeks and then stayed with another family for about three months. In the process, he continued to destroy the interiors of homes and was fond of escaping. One day when Riley was a little over two years of age, Celinda announced that we were getting Riley back, and it could possibly be for a long time. The first day Riley returned, he showed he was still a "bark star;" he seemed to bark loudly about sixteen hours a day. He appeared to be the ultimate curse of Ono. All he was good for was chasing tennis balls up and down the hills for hours. What good can come of that? Riley quickly became the straw that stirred the kennel as he could get the entire outside kennel fired up with incessant barking. After he started barking, they all barked nonstop. He didn't like to listen, either, as he was used to having his way. We started working with him, but it was going to take time. He was uncommonly strong and smart for a male dog. Very smart. Too smart, and we got the blame for breeding him.

However, everyone has a boss. Cricket, Riley's dam, used to amuse us by dragging Riley in the kennel run by the scruff of his neck while he was on his back. She would drag him a few feet, pause, and take him a distance of twenty to twenty-five feet over the span of a minute or two. He tolerated all of this even at the age of two or three because this was his mother.

Outside of fetching tennis balls—which exhausted my right arm and required that I also throw left handed—his favorite game was to go out in the far field and start digging so that his front legs, face, and chest were almost completely brown or dark brown. He looked proud of himself; the dirtier he was able to get, the happier he seemed. This meant another bath, and that could take hours.

Once he was done with his bath, he started barking; he was warmed up from his bath and attention-getting dirt-digging behavior. Once he dug so deeply in the far field that he found an underground stream. I praised him for that and thought this dog may be of some worth yet. For about a year and a half, the whole kennel operation seemed to revolve around Riley. Where was he, what has he done, why can't he be quieter? I did not foresee that he would become Riley, the superstar. But Riley always seemed to have a plan. You could watch him and imagine his brain cells working as he seemed to be planning ahead. He couldn't be rushed, though, as he was in charge of his own destiny.

Early on, we took him to a few shows out of the area. I remember the Lompoc, California, shows where we had big plans for Riley. We had a chance to see the Stevensons again, so we went. Riley didn't show at all for us and acted disinterested and tired. What a show dog! He did win a few Bests of Breed, including one of the Rose City Classic Shows in January of 2004 (in which he showed up on Animal Planet or Discovery Channel reruns for three years), but he looked like a puppy and just wouldn't keep his tail and ears up in the ring. Riley continued to look like a puppy until he turned eight or nine. I had never seen a Sam like that.

At the SCA National Show in Riverside, California, in 2003, Riley was already a champion and may have made one cut in the Best of Breed ring, but he didn't go further. For the experienced junior handler who shows very successfully today in another breed, Riley ended up sixth out of six early in the morning in Junior Handling competition—just before Saturday's Best of Breed judging. Kellyn pronounced Riley the worst show dog she had ever tried to show as he did nothing in the ring, and I remember laughing because Riley wasn't going to do a darn thing if he didn't want to. I don't think he tipped over in the ring from falling asleep, but he couldn't have been any worse and on a national stage, too. His grandfather, Travis, was notorious for falling asleep in the ring as he leaned against a bleacher, wall, or his handler.

I had to get his eyes checked every six months to see if we should keep him intact in the gene pool as he wasn't going to be bred unless he passed all the health checks. After about a year, the well-known eye specialist in Oregon suggested neutering Riley as he had punctate pinpoint cataracts. Celinda and I knew that even though the condition may be considered "breeder's choice," he had to be neutered. We had started getting inquiries regarding Riley's availability, and we knew we could do better than pass along an eye condition. Usually folks blame just the sire, but I believe it is just the unfortunate matchup of the genes of a sire and dam. Seattle had a frozen semen implant from Ono, and there were no eye problems in that litter.

Once Riley was neutered, he immediately calmed down and stopped a lot of the bad boy behavior, including the obnoxious barking. He wasn't going to be shown anymore except as a veteran at age seven at local specialties and at age eight for the National Samoyed Club of America Specialty. That was a long way off.

Riley gained a few pounds from his new sedentary lifestyle and became a therapy dog with Seattle. They both visited the Longview-Kelso assisted living and memory care facilities every Christmas Day for many, many years. Riley also helped bring up the puppies in subsequent litters, excelled at herding, and did rig and sled work periodically. Basically though, he became a couch potato. At one point he was up to nearly seventy-four pounds. I took him into the school classrooms a few times, and he seemed content just to follow anyone around inside the house and watch some TV. He liked to chase his tennis balls, squirrels, and sheep. If it moved, it was his.

When visitors came in the house, Riley approached them cheerfully with a proud swagger. He thought he was something; we had no idea of what was to come. But he always could move like the wind with never a false or awkward step. He used to go into crates sometimes, and I would tell him to get out. Without losing a beat, he would reverse himself and come out backwards without putting a foot down wrong. I thought he could have been a dancer. He was breathtaking in his movement.

When Celinda left the house to live up in Enumclaw, Washington, during the fall of 2009, I had five Samoyeds to entertain me and be my own personal therapy dogs. Riley was a little over nine years old when I sent him with Wayne Stenlund to the Washington State Samoyed Club Specialty Show in August 2010. It was his sixth show in about five years. I remember telling Wayne that Riley looked good enough to do some damage in the ring. I had been running with him in order to get him and myself in shape after my cancer surgery in 2009, and in 2008, he had started showing just at the two local specialties each year. I think Celinda had taken him to one training class in five years as he knew his ring pattern and always had his movement. I had practiced with him once a year as I couldn't really improve on anything with him. I certainly didn't want to mess him up. He was a diamond waiting to be uncovered.

For the Enumclaw Specialty in August 2010, Riley took Best of Opposite Sex, despite being neutered and without whiskers. A new handler had shaved off all his whiskers. She didn't know that we do not shave whiskers off of the Samoyeds. Dogs need them for the same reason cats need whiskers. It takes a good six months for them to grow back. The judge still put him up.

In November 2010, while talking with Heather Kelly by phone, we decided to show Riley at California specialties to "see what he could do." I was going through a divorce at the time, and pretty much all of the show expenses had stopped as Celinda was the one who had liked the travel and the three to four day show clusters out of the area. I wanted to show some of the same expenses as before for the divorce attorneys and the court. Riley was "drafted," and it is fair and correct to say that without the divorce, Riley would not have been "specialed." To "special" a dog means he or she is competing for Breed wins. As a neutered male, Riley could only be shown at Samoyed Specialty shows (there aren't that many compared to All-Breed shows), and he had to be entered in a Veteran Dog class. He had to win that class first, and then he could move up for Best of Breed judging. So, good things can come out of a mess. My cancer had started to come back, but I couldn't tell anyone. I had a show career to take care of, and Riley took us on a ride!

Riley was driven by friends and handlers down to California twice and Arizona once within a five month period. Heather said he was always in the final group for Best of Breed and did win an Award of Merit at the Phoenix Specialty. Northern California had back-to-back specialties in June of 2011 and I was feeling lucky.

I drove Riley down to Vallejo, California, and paid for Ryann Grady to fly down from Seattle to handle Riley. After I groomed Riley in the Oakland, California airport parking lot, Ryann's plane arrived, and we drove to the show. In the Best of Breed ring there were five or six of the top ten highest ranked U.S. Samoyeds for 2011. Most of the power was in the ring that night, including Cami who had won a Group One that afternoon and her sister Jett who would go on to win the 2012 SCA National. I remember looking at the dogs in the ring, wondering what I was thinking to believe I would have a chance. Ryann later told me over dinner around 11:00 p.m. that she had never won a specialty. With darkness approaching and Riley cruising only three-quarters speed, the judge gave him Best of Breed. I asked Ryann to do it again the next day, and she said nothing like pressure, Jim, with a ten-year-old veteran! Riley took Best of Opposite Sex the next night, trotting at full speed to show off those long legs as Jett won the Specialty. I liked Cami so much from the beginning that I ended up with her as my new Samoyed in August 2015.

Riley was in superb shape from running up forty-five degree hills every single day for nearly half a year. He hadn't become magically fit by accident. We had done interval training. I imagined a lot of the handlers in the Sammy ring wouldn't have been able to take that hill on a run, but Riley and I did it. We had to be better and stronger to compete at "our age." My right knee was sore sporadically for years after Riley's SCA 2011 National, but it was definitely worth the price.

The SCA National was coming up in October 2011 in Utah, but Riley had a horrible orange hot spot on his front left leg. I had to put three inner tube collars on him for a few months to keep him from chewing the spot and borrowed a Malamute-sized collar from my friend Wayne Stenlund. Walt Herrmann was judging Veteran Sweepstakes, and we had had our battles back and forth on the Samoyed Club of America (SCA) Board, so I figured Riley would be first out of the gate as soon as he showed up in the ring. I filled out the entries for the week of the National and didn't initially enter him in Sweeps. It was more money down the drain if I had to stay home with Riley's hot spot, which was orange and the size of a quarter at the time the entries were sent in. Then I thought more about Sweeps. This was Riley's last National (he had only been to one other as a champion in 2003), so he might as well "max out" and give it his best shot. I tore open the envelope for the entry and added in Sweepstakes; I wrote a second check for the Sweepstakes entry and mailed both checks in a new envelope. As it turned out, Riley needed the visibility afforded by winning Best of Opposite Sex in Veterans' Sweeps under Walt. This energized his fan club, and being a veteran was to his advantage as vets are given a round of applause when gaited in the ring, whereas the non-vet champions aren't individually applauded. This is just an unwritten rule. Riley needed everything he could get going his way, but he especially needed to get that hot spot cleared up.

On the way out to Bountiful, Utah, Riley and I hit a storm during which the sky turned black in the early afternoon. Heavy rain, ice, and hail started falling, and lightning and thunder appeared very close by. I had to pull off the road as I couldn't see more than a few feet in front of myself while driving. I thought it was a providential sign that something unexpected would happen at the show.

Once I arrived at the host hotel in Utah, I made sure to show off Riley whose hair needed combing. He had been bathed and dried the day before, but there had been no time for line combing. He didn't look like much of a threat to anyone, so I didn't have to hide him. That would come later.

On Monday, I met Leon and Kathy Ward in one of the arenas where they held Agility and Obedience. Leon and Kathy had driven out to their first National since Ono's passing in 2001. The stars and planets were continuing to align. On Tuesday, they were at the ringside when Riley won Best of Opposite Sex in the Veterans' Sweepstakes competition. At the conclusion of the event, Jane Stevenson was the first to recognize that something special might be coming up when Jane remarked that Riley "was pushing for Breed," which was later in the week. I asked Jane what she meant by her comment. She said Ono had "it" and Riley had just enough of "it" to win. I kept all of this to myself at the show site but did talk to Celinda and a few other close friends by phone; we started feeling that Riley was going to win it all on Saturday. We had convinced ourselves that there was no doubt he was going to win. For possibly the only time in my nearly twenty-five years in show dogs, I relaxed and decided to just enjoy the proceedings however it was going to play out. As my friend from New York, Tom Delaney, remarked years ago, "Nationals have a beginning and an end, and almost as if by magic, the show does go on."

Thursday came along with the competition for Best Veteran Dog in the ten to twelve year age group. Riley had to win his class under Audrey Lycan before he could move on with the other class winners to Best of Breed judging on Saturday under a different judge. If he didn't earn a first place ribbon, he would be done for the week on Thursday and could stay in the hotel room where it was cooler on Friday and Saturday, waiting for *Lone Ranger* reruns on TV. Seven dogs were entered, but Riley won the class and then had nearly a two-day wait for Saturday's show. A number of very nice veteran Sams competed in that class, and it was tough to get out of it as the winner.

On Thursday right after his win, Heather Kelly, Riley's handler, announced that she would give Riley a bath on Friday as he was moving on to the Best of Breed judging on Saturday. He needed to look his best to contend with the 119 champion Sams entered plus the class winners for the week.

The awards banquet was on Friday evening. I left at nine o'clock so I could get Riley his rest before Breed judging on Saturday. With the room cooled down to sixty-four degrees to help Riley relax, I read *The USA Today* newspaper, which featured a special travel section on Orlando. I saw "Ono's" name immediately in the letters spelling out "Orlando" and took that for another good sign. Orlando was the last place I saw Ono in 2001. I told Riley he was going to win it tomorrow.

Saturday morning came, and I remember showing Riley one of the two eight by ten inch pictures of Rex of White Way that Mardee Ward-Fanning had given me earlier in the week for my research on Rex. I put the picture in front of Riley and told him that this was his last National as he was too old to be going anymore and that he had to go out and win it for the Breed and show everyone that an old boy still could do it. In addition to his sire, Ono, he had a long history of great Sams behind him, and Rex was back there, too. I told him to go out and win it for Rex and Ono and take his place in the history books. Riley looked up at me and seemed to understand his mission. He looked at me as though he was going to do it, and I never doubted that he would.

At Best of Breed judging on Saturday, Riley was still standing tall after about six cuts. At some point early in the day, I had written "Mr. Best in Show" on the back of Riley's armband number 145. Heather didn't know this. It seemed that every time I spotted him in the ring, the sun was shining on him. I remember looking at him and thought I could see Ch. Yurok of White Cliff or sometimes the great Eng. Ch. Kara Sea standing tall. He seemed to take on different looks. Before the second or third cut, the judge told Heather that she wasn't going to make the veteran do another down and back. Heather replied, "Are you kidding? He could do this all day," and off they went.

At almost the very end of the judging, Judge Beth Riley pulled out Riley and Heather and instructed Heather to take Riley out and "do something with him." Heather took Riley on a small half circle and put him back in line. Lou Torres said to me at that point, "He's got it now." Then Judge Riley pulled Riley and put him up front, and the other Sams who were still under consideration were lined up behind him. She then pointed to Riley and proclaimed him Best of Breed for the 2011 SCA National Specialty Show! After about five owners and taking over ten years and seven months to grow up, Riley showed that he had enough of "it" to win as the oldest Samoyed to ever win a Samoyed Club of America National Specialty. Heather picked up Riley, kissed him, and carried him out of the ring, forgetting about her long-term painful back from a gymnastics injury.

Handshakes, congratulations, and hugs were followed by pictures with the team that made it possible. The next morning, I got up with Riley at 4:00 a.m. and decided to leave Utah quickly before they changed their minds. We were on the road by 5:00 a.m.

Newspaper articles and advertisements followed, and Riley joined in a walking parade in downtown Woodland. He continued his Christmas Day tradition of visiting the assisted living, independent living, and Alzheimer's home residents in Longview, Washington. He made ten or eleven Christmas Day therapy dog visits in his almost fourteen-year lifetime. He also went to Meet the Breed events at the Rose City Classic in Portland and the Clackamas shows, proving to be a fine Samoyed ambassador. He continued his sheep herding at Brigands for a number of years, and at the age of thirteen was rated "Excellent" in the basic instinct test—even though he was still feeling the effects of being sedated for his teeth cleaning the day before. He could do just about anything I asked of him.

Any time the refrigerator door opened or I stopped to pick blue berries or black berries while out walking the property, Riley would stop and automatically open his mouth like a huge lion waiting for food to be dropped or thrown in. The response when near any food was to open his mouth very wide and wait to be thrown dog biscuits, turkey, chicken, ham, carrots, broccoli, strawberries, blackberries, blue berries, or plums without seeds. He didn't wait to have the food presented first to open his mouth as he signaled with his mouth that he was ready as soon as he knew I was near food. Even stuff he couldn't have. He was proud of his skills and his little beggar routine made me laugh every day.

While doing a book signing for the *Rex of White Way* book with Riley at the Orchards Assisted Living facility in June 2013 in Brush Prairie, Washington, I was asked what my next book would be about. I hadn't really given it any thought. I paused a few seconds and heard myself saying, "It will be about my service in Vietnam." I made a public commitment, and Riley was my witness, too.

Over time, my cancer residuals started to come back, and Riley was also slowing down during the summer of 2014. I began my thirty-five prostate bed cancer radiation sessions in October 2014 at Oregon Health and Science University (OHSU) in

Portland. Riley was my companion up to the last week of radiation with his twice-a-day walks in my fruit tree and flower garden area. We had stopped running the hill in the late spring when he was slowing down. The walks were good for me and also Riley as they kept both of us moving. Finally, a few days before Thanksgiving, I made a decision that had to be made to help Riley to the Rainbow Bridge. He had taken me to the end of radiation and had done his job. What a wonderful life he had lived—oh, that all dogs should be so lucky! He retired undefeated after his 2011 SCA National win in Utah. Having won at age ten years and seven months, he remains the oldest Samoyed ever to win an SCA National Specialty show. As Amelia Price commented, perhaps Riley broke the "glass ceiling," opening the way for other veteran Samoyeds to win specialties and nationals more frequently. Ch. Wolf River's Terra had managed the feat back in Mars, PA in 1992 at the age of almost ten at that year's SCA National, and Ch. Celticfrost All Tuckered Out from Canada later won the 2014 SCA National at the age of nine.

After Riley's passing, the house seemed uncommonly quiet. I still had Honor (Riley's half sister) with me, but Riley wasn't around to "stir the pot." Or was he? The first night after helping Riley go to sleep at the veterinarian's office, I noticed the hallway motion sensor light by my downstairs bedroom going on and off, but Honor was with me in the bedroom lying on her pillow, and no one else was in the house. Then I thought it was Riley coming back to check on me. The sensor light flickering went on for about two weeks. It was actually comforting, and it wasn't every night. It finally stopped.

On the second night after Riley's passing, I was awakened around midnight by a noise in the bedroom upstairs. Someone was hitting or knocking on the sliding glass door leading into the bedroom. I had the flashlight with me and didn't recall ever hearing that kind of noise during the twelve years I had lived in the house. I opened the sliding glass door, paused a few seconds, and looked out on the deck but could find nothing as the cause of the noise. I went back to bed, and that was the end of that kind of noise for the evening. The next morning I thought it could have been Riley who was out on the deck and needed to be let in.

Over the next few weeks, pictures of Riley would tumble and fall down on the carpet from where they had been displayed. Sometimes I thought it was Honor's doing, but it was always Riley's show pictures, except one time Rex of White Way's picture was turned over. Once Riley's picture fell off the wall down by the fireplace. I still don't know how he reached that one if it was Riley's doing.

There have been no further unexplained noises or incidents of Riley's pictures falling since about two to three weeks after he died. Except that after I finished drafting Riley's chapter in this book, the late afternoon wind blew in, slamming a door. Then Riley's Best in Show picture from the Utah 2011 SCA National fell off the wall and hit the carpet with a loud thud. I think Riley is still here quietly watching, and maybe that's why I never went through a mourning period after his death. I called him the "Great One," but as Sammy owners know, all of our Sammies are special treasures or "Great Ones." He did retire, though, at the top as "Mister Best in Show."

Riley and Heather pictured right after winning the 2011 SCA National in Utah. Riley knew what he had done. Courtesy Heather Kelly.

Heather and Riley flying high at the 2011 SCA National. Courtesy Heather Kelly.

Judge Beth Riley, the Author, Heather and Riley, Bob Sencenbaugh-SCA President. Courtesy Heather Kelly.

Judge, Riley with Alan Stevenson, Celinda, Christie Smith as Riley started to grow up. Courtesy Celinda Cheskawich.

Riley and Alan taking Best of Breed. Courtesy Celinda Cheskawich.

Head study of Riley. Courtesy Celinda Cheskawich and Dan Hogan Photography.

Riley looking like he wants to now take these dog shows seriously as he is running out of time. Author's Collection.

Early show career picture with Riley and Heather, Celinda, Alan, Christie. Courtesy Celinda Cheskawich.

Ono and his Son, Riley with Alan and Heather. Courtesy Celinda Cheskawich.

Samantha surveying her back yard in Springfield, Virginia. Author's collection.

Chapter 4

Samantha Cotton Candy

Samantha Cotton Candy was my first Samoyed. I obtained her from a "backyard breeder" in 1991 by looking for puppies for sale in *The Washington Post*. I had previously owned a Samoyed-Golden Retriever mixed breed female, Bos'n, who had passed away from bladder cancer, and I wanted a purebred Samoyed of my own. Samantha had "Champions" in her distant background, but neither her dam nor sire was a show dog. I didn't really know what a show dog was at that point and knew nothing about dog shows.

I took Samantha to obedience classes the first year, but she wasn't as reliable as the other dogs with whom we practiced. Someone convinced me to go to a dog show and meet people who knew about Samoyeds and maybe join a local club so I could learn how to handle a Samoyed. I was given good advice. I never put a single point on Samantha in two years of dog shows, but I did get a reserve once under former NYC Rockette and silent picture star, Lena Basquette, who almost gave her the point but after some delay awarded it to the other Sam. I remember Lena saying that every dog has its day, but today was not my dog's day. I wanted that point and learned I wasn't very good at showing or grooming. I then took handling classes under George Alston. I think I took it twice and also went to walk-in classes located throughout Fairfax County, Virginia.

At my first dog show as an exhibitor, I approached Andrew Green who was busy preparing a Samoyed for the show for a client. I asked him why my Sam didn't look like other Sams? I had paid to have Samantha groomed at a local groomer, but we had been unable to remove the yellow. Andrew helped me by combing Samantha and gave me good grooming advice for future shows. I did make a number of close friends in the dog show world through Samantha, and in 1992 I joined the Potomac Valley Samoyed Club and soon after became their treasurer. Within a few years, I was on the audit committee for the Samoyed Club of America (SCA), and then I served the parent club as treasurer for a number of years. I became president in 1999. Along the way, I took Samantha wherever and whenever I travelled, and she proved to be a great ambassador. I continued to learn all I could about the breed because Samantha was a challenge. She continued to turn up her nose at obedience practice.

I remember visiting my sister in Salisbury, Maryland, for a week in the early 1990s and taking close to seventy-five back issues of the *Samoyed Quarterly* and the *SCA Bulletin* with me. Most of these were obtained for about fifty cents a magazine from auctions at "Camp Gone to the Dogs" in Putney, Vermont. I read everything I could on the breed and couldn't get enough. I thought I was reading way too much, but I came to realize early on that I was hooked, and we should all have passions like this. I even had Ross Chapin run a pedigree search on Samantha so I could look at all the champions behind her—although they didn't start showing up in her pedigree for a few generations. I was really impressed with those early dogs who were the twelve key dogs of the breed as we know it today. I became immersed in the history of the breed, which eventually led me to writing Rex's book and then setting up The Rex of White Way Samoyed Memorial Library and Museum.

As for Samantha, she definitely didn't like Obedience, probably didn't like Conformation dog shows, and didn't like practicing for anything more than once. But she did like sheep. I took Samantha up to "Camp Gone to the Dogs" in Putney, Vermont, for the first time in 1992. There she met the sheep. We also discovered she liked swimming, lure coursing, most of the agility equipment, sometimes sledding, hunting, and anything new the first time. She was bored if we had to do anything twice. I remember the lure coursing and how, from the holding area, she watched other dogs run the pattern set out on a large athletic field. She started cutting corners her second try on a course. Each day's course was new. She used to run across the field to the exit to wait for the plastic white bag to come around. After that first day, she wouldn't give an honest run ever again although she went to Camp for almost six years, and the course always changed. She anticipated the course and didn't play fair. I think sometimes she even remembered the previous year's course. I could see her ears and head move to follow the white plastic lure and almost imagine what she was thinking and planning. She was just too smart and was a true Samoyed. Fool me once, but you won't get away with it again.

When duck hunting, she ran for the downed duck the second time and disappeared over a hill into a far field with the duck in her mouth. I had to run her down for a few minutes—she was headed into Massachusetts if I didn't catch her. Swimming was pretty easy and a lot of fun. For the first time on the sled hookup with Alan Katz, she wasn't so sure. Because of her inexperience, she wasn't able to always keep up with the conditioned and trained athletes, so we kept it slow. Later on, she used to run with Rebel and General when doing rig work or sled work whenever we got about four to six inches of snow at Accotink Park near Fairfax, Virginia.

Out of all of this exposure to what a Sammy could do at "Camp Gone to the Dogs," I decided to back off the shows and take up sheep herding with her. We often practiced three times a week on sheep at a farm in Philomont, Virginia. Samantha earned her Pre-Trail level title on sheep and was one of the first ten Samoyeds to earn that title. I believe she was the second Samoyed bitch to earn a Pre-Trial title on sheep. In one match she nearly completed a run comparable to the first leg of Herding Started but ended up with a disqualification for stopping too long to do her business just before she was about to complete a nice run.

Samantha was my introduction into the world of Samoyeds, Samoyed history, and being an officer with local and national dog clubs. She lived to be almost twelve, and during the last six months of her life, she stayed with Christie and Dale Smith, playing queen of the house—a role she loved. My next dog, though, was going to be a show dog, and that led to General who had a long line of champions on both sides.

General (L) and Samantha (R) with their boots on. Author's collection.

General (L) and Samantha (R) at Camp Gone to the Dogs in the Early 1990's. Author's collection.

Chapter 5

General and His Gift to Me

A Newfound Appreciation for U.S. and World History

General (Romsey's Gen'l Stonewall Jax'n) came from a well-known breeder in Jackson, Mississippi. I needed a good name for him and wanted "Jackson" to be a part of it to show where the dog came from. We already had a "Sir Paws Gen'l Lee" in the Samoyed ring in Virginia, and I felt he needed a partner. I asked my supervisor at work about a "General Jackson" I vaguely remembered from my passing studies, and he immediately loaned me a new popular biography of General Stonewall Jackson, which I read quickly and with much interest as I needed a Samoyed with a name that stood for greatness.

Reading the first biography of a Civil War general on my own and without worrying about a grade for my efforts seemed strange at first and reminded me of how engrossed I used to be reading the biographies of Babe Ruth, Mel Ott, Lou Gehrig, and Christy Mathewson while growing up. Stonewall Jackson was an eccentric genius whose battle plans and maneuvers in the Shenandoah Valley during the Civil War are still studied at West Point. In one notable series of battles, Jackson was outnumbered almost eight to one—yet the troops under his command took on four different union armies attacking, defeating, and retreating. How could this be possible?

This was how history finally came alive for me, and I thank the Samoyed dog world! When I substitute teach in the classroom, I tell the students how I finally found history enjoyable, meaningful, and useful. I became hooked on history and the Civil War, which I had previously avoided in my studies. Going to dog shows in Virginia, Pennsylvania, and Maryland also led me to visit Civil War battlefields as they were easily accessible. I even found the farm where Jackson's left arm is supposedly buried along with a primitive sign. In the cold of winter, I later visited the memorial cemetery in Lexington, Virginia, and saw lemons on his grave to celebrate his birthday on January 21. The Virginia Military Institute cadets never forget that Stonewall liked his lemons.

After studying Stonewall Jackson, I read biographies of J.E.B. Stuart, then Robert E. Lee, and then Ulysses S. Grant. From that foundation, it was easy to go into

Rommel, Ike and Truman, William O. Douglas, Robert McNamara, General Douglas MacArthur, the Kennedy Dynasty, The Bush Family, and *Master of the Senate* (LBJ); finally I read *1776* about General George Washington. Years later while in England to attend three days of the world's largest dog show, Cruft's, I visited Heaver Castle, saw Winston Churchill's home, and began to read biographies of Henry VIII, Anne Boleyn, and Elizabeth I. On my trip to England in 2017, I visited more castles, Canterbury Cathedral, and Runnymede—the site of the Magna Carta signing in 1215. In 2018, visits are planned for the Scottish Highlands and maybe meeting my distant cousins from the Ross and MacKenzie clans who were supporters of Mary Queen of Scots. (Coincidently, the author of Part II of this book, Annie Reid, is a direct descendant of Mary Queen of Scots.)

So, after reading over a half dozen biographies of Stonewall Jackson, I was sure my General was special and was going to win big at every dog show. General was on the small size but still within the breed standard. However, he never quite developed the big chest I expected and never won a single point in the Conformation ring. He did earn a reserve at a Manassas show one year, and I thought that was a given since his namesake, Stonewall Jackson, had distinguished himself twice at Manassas/Bull Run during Civil War battles.

General was a happy boy and was a playmate for Samantha. Compared to some others, General wasn't the cleverest Sammy, but maybe he was the happiest. As I have shared with the stories of Riley and others, a very smart boy with nothing to keep him occupied will just get into trouble again and again. General was a delight to be around, and even when he barked, he wasn't obnoxious but instead had a dignified bark. He was a southern gentleman Samoyed.

Once, while reading one of the many Stonewall Jackson biographies, I stopped to throw small dog biscuit treats up in the air for Samantha and General. Samantha caught her treat and then caught General's, too, while he wasn't looking. Poor General looked around for hours for that treat. He expected it to come down, but it never did. I provided other treats that evening, but General was fixated on the one that got away.

Samantha usually pulled tricks on General, and he was left getting blamed for something she had done. I used to wonder how General got so dirty on his chest and head while his paws were clean. After weeks of trying unsuccessfully to figure out the mystery, I observed Samantha throwing dirt with her front paws between her standing back legs right at General who was sometimes standing directly behind her. I watched him take the dirt on his chest and head. He seemed to get some pleasure out of all of this, but all I saw was a dirty show dog who needed to be cleaned up.

Since Samantha wasn't into the sledding as much as I thought she should be, I trained General as a lead dog using Lee Fishback's book, *Training Lead Dogs*. General often worked as lead dog alongside Timber, an intact Malamute male belonging to Denise Allen, in our rig and sled work. We found good trails to work on in Fairfax County, Virginia. Denise's female, Alaska, easily weighed over one hundred pounds and usually worked in back at wheel. General was very adaptable and later took a liking to Denise's Malamute named Magic even though he was outweighed by sixty or seventy pounds. They played for hours together. Sometimes I ran General at lead with Samantha and Rebel at wheel if Denise was unable to participate. Duane Johnson sometimes brought Tana or another Sam, and we found room for all of them in harness at Lake Accotink Park or Burke Lake Park. General was the only Sam I had who knew left from right, "whoa," and "on by." He kept the line tight out front as lead dog, and that's what he was supposed to do.

I took General for our regular sheep herding lessons and sometimes chose not to work him as he wasn't always keen on the sheep. We took him for the basic instinct test, and he needed two legs to pass the AHBA test. We tried a few times, and finally he passed. It seemed that General liked to work the entire flock of forty sheep and not just the three or four we picked out for him. One time, General worked his way out of his crate and jumped out the back of the Dodge Caravan, heading off for the sheep who were a good distance away on a hill. Sue, the trainer, suggested we just let him be as he wasn't going anywhere near those sheep. General, however, found an opening through the fence and proceeded to move the sheep from one end of the field to the other on his own by weaving back and forth behind them. We went up to the field and called him to us, and he brought all forty sheep to us.

From this incident we learned that if General shut down on three or four sheep we should just turn him loose with the flock and let him herd in his own way. Once, while walking backward in the field with Sue, forty sheep, and General behind the sheep, I tripped and fell over a log. I just lost my concentration on my own safety as I was amazed at how General could work the sheep when he wanted to at just the right pace so they wouldn't bolt, yet he had enough presence that the sheep moved along in a bunch. Neither Samantha nor Rebel was given a chance to work forty sheep at once, but General showed them how to do it.

In Springfield, Virginia, I lived in a large house on almost two thirds of an acre surrounded by five foot high wooden fencing. Behind our property across Pohick Road was a fire station. General loved the sirens and flashing lights on the fire trucks, and if we didn't turn him outside to run to the end of the fence and bark at the trucks, General spent his time inside the house barking. Sometimes there would be fire alerts several times throughout the night, and General reminded us each time so we wouldn't miss the alarms.

All the Sams stayed in the house when we had company. Once while we were playing *Monopoly*, the deed for Baltic Avenue fell off the table, and General wouldn't give it up until he ate half the card. We continued to play Monopoly for many years afterwards and never tired of telling the story of how General had made the deeded property even less desirable to have.

In our drive across the U.S. after I retired from my government job in Washington, DC, in July 2002, General came with us in a crate in the back of the Ford Cargo van with five other individually crated Samoyeds. At our new home, he spent a lot of time in run number one in the outdoor kennel. Oftentimes he would join us in the house or on the deck. At some point, General struck up a friendship with the many owls who lived in the woods. The owls seemed to start their hooting whenever it got dark. We noticed that General talked back to the owls and sometimes barked to get them to talk to him. If he barked and they didn't call back, he was disappointed. When they did start to hoot back, General jumped up with joy and barked quickly in return. He had made a connection. This went on for several hours each night whether General was on the deck or in his kennel run. None of our other Sams talked to the owls like General did. He could get three or four hooting pretty quickly from different directions. This went on for many years and was a continual source of delight for Celinda and me.

General lived to be almost fifteen years old and was suffering from many health issues when I had him put down in the local veterinarian's office while I held him in my arms. I remember bringing him back home that day during a light snowfall in the early afternoon. I dug a hole with my shovel and buried him along the side of the kennel, and Celinda placed several owl figurines on top of his burial spot. Almost immediately, dozens of owls appeared to begin their mourning serenade. This went on for several hours, beginning before darkness set in, which was unusual. Celinda and I knew he had made a special connection with the owls, and this was further proof. It continued to snow, and it snowed for three days almost nonstop. The Chinese stock market crashed the day General was put in the ground, and the owls disappeared for several years after their vain attempts to call for him. Where they went I do not know. Why they went was because they had lost their General. After several years had passed, an owl could occasionally be heard on the property, but the large choir was gone for good with the death of its choirmaster. General still has his owl figurines on his gravesite.

General on the right and Samantha on the left as lead dogs. A borrowed neighbor's dog was at wheel with the Author on the sled. Author's collection.

General was a happy boy. Author's collection.

Chapter 6

Noah

Noah (Ch. d'Keta's Bronze Blessing, CGC, HCT-s) was Celinda's dog from the very beginning and was too smart for his own good. Celinda never set boundaries for Noah, and from about four months of age he was allowed to go outside on the deck anytime as Celinda had an "open door" policy with him. He seldom listened to me when I tried to show him. Noah liked to start fights with Riley—Noah wasn't so smart on those days. When a bitch was in season in the house, I once saw Noah open three doors to get to the girl within twenty seconds. He figured out everything quickly and was high energy. I used to place red pepper around and in the garbage can under the sink behind the cabinet door with the childproof latch on it. Noah just thought the pepper was another obstacle to work around and still went through the garbage can at will.

Noah finished his championship pretty easily. He made a fool of us and himself at one of the SCA Nationals, and the judge still gave him the first place ribbon in a very large class. Because he continued to act like a fool in the Winner's Dog judging of that National—playing more games, including taking the lead in his mouth as he gaited around the ring—he ruined his chances for serious consideration.

After Celinda moved out of the house, leaving me with five Samoyeds, I couldn't make any placements until all the property was divided and the attorneys were happy. At the first opportunity, we found a great home for Noah in Canada where he still thrives as the only Sam in the house. He gets worked every day to burn off all that excess energy. In a house with four other Sams, Noah fought even with his mother, Honor, and there was no peace unless I used the crates all the time. I liked to tell people that Noah was "banished to Canada," but we simply found a great home for him.

Noah and Celinda herding sheep. Courtesy Celinda Cheskawich.

Chapter 7

Seattle

Seattle (Multi-BISS Ch. d'Keta's Purple Reign, CGC, ROMC) was the dowry I received when I married Celinda in June of 1999. If Cami (see Chapter 8) is the "Princess," Seattle was the "Queen." After Celinda and I got married, Seattle stayed out on the West Coast for a while showing with her handler, Rick Baggenstos. I remember cutting the grass over a long weekend in Virginia that first summer, and Celinda came out at midday on successive days to tell me that Seattle took Breed again and a "piece of the group," and I had to send another bonus check to Rick. I told Celinda that at the rate Seattle was going, I would be broke in a few months. Seattle was an alpha girl who didn't have to fight anyone to keep the pack in line, even tough boy Noah. Maybe once a year she had to partially raise a lip to someone, but everyone knew she was in charge. If another girl was in season, and Seattle had been out of season for a few weeks, she came right back in season. No one was going to be bred unless she was first in line.

Once, she did fight with Rebel for twenty seconds over ice cubes in the living room of our Springfield, Virginia home. Although Rebel outweighed Seattle by twenty-five pounds, the match was a draw and over swiftly. She got her punches and bites in quickly. Rebel backed away and called off the fight as he knew he was outmatched in the long run against a smarter opponent.

One time, Seattle captured a squirrel in our backyard while I was working at my day job. She kept the other four Samoyeds interested but a good four to five feet away while she played with the squirrel. Celinda said Seattle had kept the live squirrel in her mouth for hours and wouldn't come in the house nor give up the squirrel until I got back from work. Then Seattle finally released the squirrel for me.

Another time, Seattle and Cricket found and played with a large, fat, ten to twelve feet long black snake until I showed up with a shovel and cut up the snake to get rid of it over the five foot high fence. Because we frequently kept the dogs outside for hours at a time in the large backyard, I don't know how long they amused themselves with the snake before I arrived to put an end to the game. Seattle could catch a bee or wasp in her mouth and kill it instantly before we knew what was going on. I think she trained her daughter Faithie to be just as quick. Squirrels, rabbits, and possums were outmatched when Seattle was on the hunt. I always kept a shovel nearby to remove the target of one of her hunting endeavors. The black snake was probably the riskiest hunt, but she could have been stung quickly by the bees. We were sure Seattle's dam had trained her to hunt well, and Seattle carried on the tradition with her offspring. If you can't hunt, you don't eat.

She spent most of her nighttime in bed sleeping on my left shoulder for seven to eight hours at a clip. She did this for almost nine or ten years. After we moved away from Washington, DC, she once fell off the bed in the middle of the night with a loud thump, and we thought it was a Northwest earthquake.

Seattle gave us six puppies in her first litter, born on St. Patrick's Day 2000. The delivery took about sixty minutes, and I assumed all litters were born this way. Even though Seattle was an outcross, five of the six puppies in her first litter became AKC Champions. She ended up producing eight AKC Champions and winning two Specialties in her show career. She was tied for first the last time I checked on which outcross bitch had produced the most champions and had also won either a Best in Show at an All-Breed Show or Best in Show at a Samoyed Specialty.

Seattle was a strong mother who kept her pups in line. The first litter was a rowdy bunch. At six weeks of age, they used to stand on their hind legs in a fenced-in area in the living room and bark throughout the night. Their mom was a "bark star," so she trained them to be like her. "Faithie," who probably most resembled her mom in the barking department, could bark nonstop for four hours, and then she was just getting warmed up for the rest of the day's barking sessions.

After the puppies were placed at ten weeks of age (we did keep Faithie for six years until she was placed with the Gustafsons in Minnesota), I started running with Seattle several times a week to get her ready for more shows. This time she would stay on the East Coast.

Her first show out of the whelping box was the Atlanta Specialty, which took place about four months after the puppies were placed. On the way down to Atlanta in September or October of 2000, I asked Celinda for almost two hours to explain to me what a "BISS" and a "BIS" meant. Celinda said I would never see one, so she saw no point in educating me. I told Celinda that I was SCA president and needed to know all these things. Particularly with me on the end of the lead, she said, it wasn't possible in my lifetime. Somehow, though, she relented and told me what I needed to know as we were setting up crates at the exhibit hall the night before the Atlanta Samoyed Specialty.

The day arrived for the big show. There were about ten specials in the ring, and Seattle won the Specialty with me on the end of the lead. Then I knew what a "BISS" felt like as well as knowing what it stood for. Winning something like that made it easy for me to see how people get hooked on the adrenaline rush from dog shows. I had waited eight years for my first Specialty win.

The SCA 2000 National Show came to Frederick, Maryland, and I ended up showing a bunch of puppies along with Seattle as Celinda was unable to show. I don't think I won any ribbons or placements, and I wasn't much of a threat to anyone with my handling skills. Seattle was one of the last two Sams cut in the Best of Breed ring, though, as I showed her. However, since I had promised not to show, judge, or campaign with paid ads if elected president, a motion came up in one of our subsequent monthly board meetings banning the president from showing at a Samoyed Club of America (SCA) National. The motion was defeated, but it wasn't a unanimous vote. I called the motion the "Seattle Motion."

During 2001, I had to show Faithie and Seattle on the Cherry Blossom Circuit as Celinda was unable to show for many months at a time due to a painful back injury. I was unable to win anything in eighteen shows. I wasn't that good. I attended more handling training classes, and Eric Liebes gave me the Most Improved Handler Award after a weekend training session in Maryland. I think he just felt sorry for me. I had nowhere to go but up. I remember Eric instructed us to get out of the way if there is a big show coming up, and you don't think you have the skills to compete. Hire a handler. That lesson stayed with me through the years and was proven true with Riley at the 2011 SCA National when Heather Kelly was drafted to show him. Eric taught me well.

The 2001 SCA National in Denver took place during my last month as president. I couldn't hear the call for Seattle's number to report for the ring, so they came to get me. I was beyond embarrassed. Seattle ended up with an Award of Merit, and as I exited the ring I noticed the person who had made the motion to bar the current president from showing at a National. She rolled her eyes upward, and I walked out with Seattle and her second Award of Merit at a National. Her first was won in 1999 with Celinda showing her.

Back at home, Seattle and Riley continued doing rig work for many years, and both did therapy dog work for many Christmas Day performances at the Longview-Kelso Assisted Living and Alzheimer Home residences. I used to watch both dogs move in front of me as I brought them back home from their rig work. I felt pretty lucky to have both at one time. They were both very special. As Joannie Luna once said, "Fame is fleeting, so enjoy it while you can as neither we nor the Sams live forever, and things happen quickly to end show careers."

Seattle won the Willamette Valley Samoyed Fanciers Specialty in 2007 as a veteran. After the show, we drove to Goldendale, Washington, to spend the weekend with all of our Sams. Unbeknownst to us, Seattle had taken a liking to cheat grass, and the fine grass blades and stems had gotten stuck on her tonsils. She was standing up in bed thrashing her head, drinking too much water, and gagging from about midnight onwards. After a sleepless and restless night for all of us, we took Seattle to the Goldendale veterinarian who discovered the problem quickly. Seattle had to be sedated and the tonsils "cleaned" while she was sleeping. She recovered, and we learned to keep all the dogs away from that stuff in the future.

Seattle had one last job to do, though, before her time was up. I was diagnosed with prostate cancer in 2008 and had radical prostate surgery in January 2009. Seattle (as well as Riley) got me up and out of the house for multiple walks each day but I wasn't strong enough to walk them both together. At one point after my surgery—while I was still hooked up with the catheter and recovering—Seattle stood up on the bed as if to say something is wrong with me, too, but I didn't know what it was. She showed nasal cancer symptoms the third week in January when she started bleeding from her nose at the Rose City Classic, and visits to the veterinarian confirmed the diagnosis. The outcome appeared certain, and we didn't have much time.

Seattle continued to be my constant companion, helping me stay busy with walks. I also helped her by keeping her moving and getting her outside for exercise as she was fighting her own cancer. The time came in March of 2009 to put her to sleep. She had seen me through my recovery from early January surgery; now I had to return the favor. She was buried in the woods next to General, facing east to guard the kennel. The bricks from Rex's playground up at the Hilltop are on top of her grave. It was a huge loss for Celinda and me, and it took a long while for both of us to recover. Seattle was a great girl!

Seattle winning Best of Breed for her first BISS with Judge Darla Cassidy at Atlanta Specialty in 2000. Courtesy Celinda Cheskawich.

*Seattle winning a Group Second Puppy with Celinda.
Courtesy Celinda Cheskawich.*

*"Sell those pork belly futures now!" Author's collection and
courtesy Beckley, WVA Mine Academy, MSHA.*

*Seattle with Ryann Grady early in her show career.
Courtesy Celinda Cheskawich.*

*Seattle and a Group I with Rick Baggenstos, Handler.
Courtesy Celinda Cheskawich.*

Seattle's First AOM at the National with Celinda, Judge Joan Luna, SCA President Amelia Price, and Show Chair Rob Barkhaus.

Group photo of Seattle and almost all her kids from the first litter. The sire is to Seattle's right with Julie Beatty. Courtesy Celinda Cheskawich.

*Seattle liked being in charge and could dress up when at the office.
Author's collection and courtesy Beckley, WVA Mine Academy, MSHA.*

Seattle (3rd from right) with some of her kids at 2003 SCA National in Riverside, California. Courtesy Celinda Cheskawich.

Chapter 8

Cami Camillia

If ever there lived a Sam who reminded me most of Seattle, Cami is the one. She has that barking routine down solidly, too. GCH-Silver Azteca's Pink Camillia came to me well credentialed with many significant wins on her resume. She had finished out 2011 as the number two Samoyed female in the country based on one system of computing win points in the show ring. She was number three Samoyed female in 2012. She already had six Group Ones when she walked through the door of my house in July of 2015 and declared that she was in charge now, and why is my lunch late?

I first saw her in 2011 when Riley went down to the Northern California (Nor Cal) Specialty in Vallejo, California, and Cami had taken a Group One in the all-breed show just prior to the evening's Nor Cal Samoyed Specialty. Some of her Group wins were over four hundred dogs in California. I also spent time with her at the Rex booth in September 2014 in Des Moines, Iowa, and asked Joannie Luna if I could have her then. However, at the time I was preparing for thirty-five upcoming radiation appointments to deal with the return of my cancer, and at the start of treatment I had been given a fifty-fifty chance to beat the disease. As I like to imagine, God flipped a coin, and it came up "heads" in my favor. My cancer was gone in May 2015, which was six months after radiation treatments had ended. So I was on my "third life," having beaten cancer twice. With Honor being a thirteen-year-old senior citizen, I asked for Cami again at the June 2015 Canby, Oregon, Show.

Cami was sent on her way to serve as my personal therapy dog, to be there for my recovery, and to see how it worked out for both of us. After taking a look at her, I decided to put her back in the ring to see what she could do at age seven. She didn't win every time—as no one does—but she quickly started racking up championship points and achieved her Grand Champion Silver in August 2015 with Select Bitch and then Best of Opposite Sex at a large show cluster in Enumclaw, Washington.

She did run up a string of five Best of Breed wins out of seven shows during the spring of 2016. I liked the dog shows again, the adrenaline rush, and seeing Cami in the Group ring. Included in the middle of that run was a Breed win with almost twenty-four Sams entered in Idaho. Cami was in season and working on a hot spot as I drove to that show. I kept her in a protective Elizabethan collar on Friday night but didn't put the collar back on immediately as I quickly brushed my teeth on Saturday morning.

Within about thirty seconds, Cami presented herself to me in the bathroom with blood dripping down her front left leg as she had reopened her hot spot. I patched her up and seriously considered going home instead of to Saturday's show. She ended up taking Breed among an entry of almost two dozen Sams, including seven Specials. About an hour before her Group was to begin, being "in season" had upset her constitution, so she had a messy backside from diarrhea. I found a goat or sheep wash in back of the show arena and hosed her off in a tub. I was able to blow dry her in time for the Group. She went to the ring, and to show how strong she was, she ran around as if nothing was going on, but I later learned that she was fighting an infection. The judge said at the photo session that she had made one of the cuts, but I was hiding so as not to upset the chemistry between the handler and Cami, and thus, I did not clearly see the ring proceedings.

Cami went to a few more shows and took a few more Breed wins but soon showed an ongoing urinary tract infection that required several rounds of antibiotics over the following few weeks. Just when we thought we were in the clear after she won two Veteran Sweepstakes in a row at the Northern California Samoyed Specialties, pyometra showed up, and she had an emergency spay operation just in time. I gave the veterinarian office my credit card and instructed them to do what they had to do to save her. They said she was almost a textbook case for open pyometra surgery, and she survived without complications. I had to take care of her with the inflatable "inner tube" on for two weeks to allow the surgical incision to heal so that she could get back to her full-time job of being my therapy dog. As with bloat, if you catch pyometra early, dogs can make a full recovery if it's not their time yet.

During her recovery, she took more naps than usual on the bed and liked to pull the covers back to lie on the sheet. Joannie called her a "princess," and that fit her perfectly. In the years ahead we have more high school football practices, book signings, and Meet the Breed Days to attend. Cami also continues her therapy dog work at the Longview Assisted Living and Alzheimer's Home as she inherited Riley's and Seattle's Christmas Day job. She is now nine and should have a long life still ahead of her.

Never underestimate a Samoyed as I am sure she has many adventures and probably a surprise show win left in her. As a spayed veteran female, she can still be shown at local Samoyed Specialties and the SCA National. Cami is now certified to fly with me in the cabin on plane trips and I don't go anywhere without her.

Cami and Rick Baggenstos taking Best of Breed under Judge Christie Smith in Idaho in 2016. Author's collection.

Left: Cami Head Study. Photo courtesy Joan Luna Liebes.

Right: Cami in backyard in Woodland, WA. Photo by author.

Cami with Joan Luna Liebes and Judge Christie Smith. Photo courtesy Joan Luna Liebes.

*Cami at the show with Joan Luna Liebes.
Photo courtesy Joan Luna Liebes.*

Cami and Mike Stone with a Group Placement. Courtesy Joan Luna Liebes.

Cami and Mike Stone with a Group One. Courtesy Joan Luna Liebes.

Cami in Texas. Photo courtesy Joan Luna Liebes.

Cami on the California circuit with handler. Photo courtesy Joan Luna Liebes.

Cami growing up with Joan Luna Liebes. Courtesy Joan Luna Liebes.

One of six Group One's for Cami. Pictured here with handler, Mike Stone. Photo courtesy Joan Luna Liebes.

Cami at the show. Photo courtesy Joan Luna Liebes.

Cami at the 2017 National as a veteran with Dr. Eric Liebes. Courtesy Joan Luna Liebes.

*Cricket winning a Group Two with Celinda under Judge Esporite.
Courtesy Celinda Cheskawich*

*Cricket becoming a New Champion with Celinda. She is Riley's Dam.
Courtesy Celinda Cheskawich.*

Chapter 9

Cricket

As Riley's dam, Cricket (Ch. Sanorka's Trip Into Tamara) has her own place in the record book for producing the 2011 SCA National Specialty winner. I remember her as a dog who was very special to me. She was the first Samoyed I put points on in the show ring as she won her second major at a show in Maryland. She also took Best of Breed that day, beating Seattle (who was out of coat) and possibly other specials in the ring at the time. After about forty (or was it fifty?) shows with multiple Samoyeds, I finally won a point as a handler! I may have the dubious record for dog show futility.

A few weeks later at another Maryland show, Cricket took Breed with Celinda handling her. She also earned a Group Two in tough Working Group competition. She retired very soon thereafter and became a brood bitch in March 2001. When Riley was born, she needed a C-section because Riley was blocking a normal delivery. She is the only one that Riley used to listen to for the first few years of his life. Cricket dragged Riley on his back from one end of the kennel run to the other. She did this almost every day while the two shared a kennel run.

"Cricky" gave us two more nice litters through normal delivery (there was no Riley to slow down the process), and when we needed to downsize the group of Samoyeds in the house, we found a wonderful home for Cricket in Canada where she lived out her last few years until she died of bloat. She opened up the "Northwest Passage," which also allowed us to place Mister Noah later on when he got too big for his britches.

Rebel winning Best of Breed with Sue Dye handling. Author's Collection.

Chapter 10

Rebel

Back during the time when I owned only Samantha and General, and I still hadn't won anything in the Conformation ring, I found "Ch. Moonsong's Gmbl'r JEB Stuart," otherwise known as Rebel. As with my first two Samoyeds, I couldn't put a single point or win on Rebel because he wouldn't listen to me. I wasn't skilled enough as a handler to get him to show. His co-breeder, Cindy, showed him easily to his championship—winning back to back five point majors to do it.

I started sheep herding with Rebel when he was around seven months of age. He took many tumbles, and I am certain now, looking back, that he ruined his hips for the OFA exams he took later at ages two and three. When he had a preliminary hip evaluation at six or seven months, he looked good, but the sheep herding lessons—often two to three times a week for eighteen to twenty-four months—took their toll.

But he could herd! We skipped the basic instinct and pretrial tests, going right ahead to the Herding Started course. Without much difficulty, he became one of the first ten Samoyeds to have a Pre-Trial or Herding Started title on him. One weekend he won Best of Breed at a show, and the next weekend he competed and won a leg in Herding Started. He looked very handsome on the course with his show groom, and he knew his commands well.

With showing and herding I had a versatile Samoyed. He took a number of Breed wins in tough East Coast competitions, and he sometimes beat top five or top ten Samoyeds in the ring. After the National one year, I invited Janice and Richie Hovelmann to a farm in Connecticut as Rebel was a "sure thing" to get his second leg, and that would earn his Herding Started title. We brought along expensive champagne and snacks to celebrate. We were all excited to be on the doorstep of having one of the first half dozen or so Samoyeds to first obtain an AKC Herding Started title.

The "Rebster" lasted all of twenty-five seconds before he was disqualified for pinning two or three sheep up against the fence and for not coming back to his handler. As Janice and Richie quickly drove away, I remember Janice saying, "You made me drive out of the way for *this!*"

"Rebbie" acquired his second leg very easily on the next opportunity. He was shown a little bit longer in the Conformation ring and was neutered at age three. He was placed back with Cindy and Bill at around age four. Celinda and I had too many Sams in the house at that point, and there was too much commotion with big Rebel getting into spats with the other Sams, especially General. My friend Denise Allen was convinced General started these fights. Rebel lived to be almost fourteen and was a better-behaved boy in a home without General.

Chapter 11

Purple Girl

Purple Girl (Grand Ch. d'Keta's Sassy Bronze Dancer) was out of Honor's last litter in March 2006. She was the last to be born in Honor's third litter and came out more dead than alive. Linda Martinson worked very hard trying to get the newborn to breathe, but I had to take her to the Vancouver Emergency Clinic twenty-five minutes away to save her. After thirty minutes of emergency procedures for a newborn, the veterinarian came out with an x-ray to report that they could save her, but the cost would be in four figures. I looked at the perfectly formed vertebrae and without hesitation went for life. After special nursing needs that lasted for a few weeks, she joined her siblings and quickly caught up to them. She was placed in a show home.

In a short period of time, she ended up an AKC Champion, a brood bitch, and winner of Best of Opposite Sex at the Arizona Samoyed Specialty among an entry of ninety. In tandem with her daughter, she earned over ten Best Brace in Show wins. The high point of her show career was winning a Group Two at an All-Breed Show in 2016 as she approached the age of eleven.

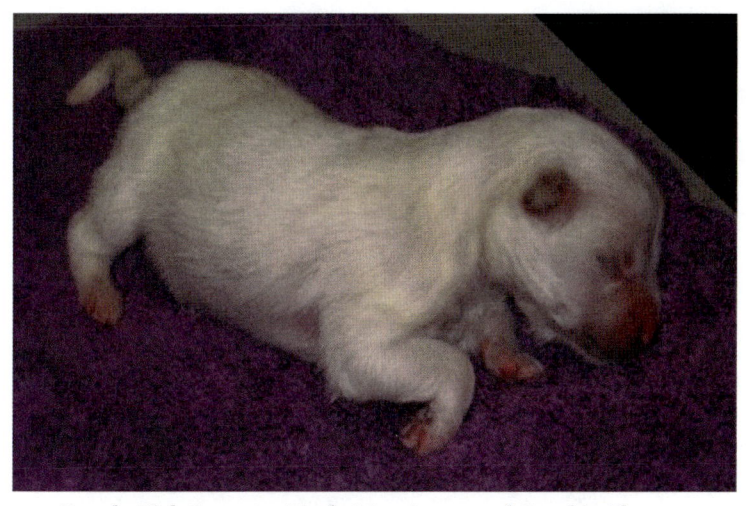

Purple Girl. Courtesy Linda Martinson and Cynthia Fleenor.

Pictures of Purple Girl. Courtesy Linda Martinson and Cynthia Fleenor.

Chapter 12

Madelin Druse

This story is about a special dog person who gave much to the Samoyed breed. I was introduced to Madelin while researching stories and anecdotes about Rex of White Way. We met by phone in 2004 through probably Joannie Luna or Alice Lombardi and stayed in touch periodically through emails and phone calls. Madelin wrote a very nice endorsement for the Rex book that appears on the back outside jacket of Rex's story. While I worked on the Vietnam book in 2013 and 2014 and did more marketing for Rex's book, we became closer. Madelin had a wealth of Samoyed knowledge acquired from exhibiting, sledding, breeding, judging, and doing many parades with her Samoyeds. She was a mentor to many in the breed and maintained a unique historical collection of photos, trophies, newspaper clippings, journals, pedigree books, ribbons, and spinning wheels, as well as Samoyed vests, sweaters, coats, and hats.

In the spring and summer of 2015, incurable cancer took its hold, causing her to deteriorate rapidly. She was transferred to hospice care for the last week or two before she died. We stayed in touch by telephone and sometimes I sent her fresh flowers. She wanted the Samoyed treasures to go to the Rex Library and her collection of very old musical instruments to go to Linfield College in Oregon. Any extra Samoyed trophies were to go to the Northern California Samoyed Club. She wanted her ashes scattered in Bandon, Oregon.

I told Madelin I would visit her in hospice care in Redding, California, for the first time in person on August 3, 2015. When I drove to Redding that morning, being unfamiliar with the town, I got lost on the way to her storage units and later at her hospice care facility. By around 11:00 a.m., I had located the correct building but still didn't know which of the two patients in the room was Madelin. After getting confirmation from the nurse's station that Madelin was the first patient in the room and being advised that she was very sick and would die soon, I reappeared in her room. I stood by her side, took her still warm hand, and announced, "I am Jim Cheskawich from Woodland, Washington, and I am glad to finally meet you in person." At that point, Madelin gave a soft sigh and immediately died as I held her hand. I said a prayer for her, left the room to find the nurse, and told the nurse what had happened. It took a few weeks, but Madelin's will in which she had left instructions to donate Samoyed collectibles to the Rex Library and musical instruments to Linfield College was determined by a Redding attorney to be invalid.

Tania Kaylor (Madelin's daughter) and I eventually worked out all of the details, and the Rex Library received Madelin's unique Samoyed collection within a few months, Linfield received its musical treasures (including a French oboe from around 1905) in January 2016, and the Northern California Samoyed Club received the extra specialty trophies. Madelin's gift to me was that she trusted me; her spirit waited until I met her, and then she knew her job was done and it was "ok" to let go. Her ashes were scattered, as she requested, in the fall of 2016 in Bandon, Oregon. She was a great lady and the Breed owes much to her for her work for the Samoyed.

Madelin Druse winning under Judge Bob Ward. Courtesy Madelin Druse Collection.

Chapter 13

Honor

Ch. d'Keta Honors Onyx (Honor) always seemed content to stay in the background and didn't try to compete with Seattle, Riley, or Cami for top dog status. She knew her station in life as a supporting cast member and team player. In a sense, she always "ran under the radar" as she fit in with the pack and didn't cause troubles or ever get sick until her last day. She finished her brief show career at ten months of age in three shows. She never saw the Conformation ring again but became a brood bitch at around age two.

Growing up, she was a picky eater, and I fed her for several years with a plastic spoon and moistened kibble while I stood and hunched over her to put the food in her mouth. I had learned this trick earlier when feeding The General. Even when she was nursing her first litter, Honor didn't like to eat anything on her own except vanilla ice cream.

She was a faithful companion and watchdog in her long life and would not tolerate a cat coming within a thousand feet of the yard.

When I started my cardiac rehabilitation in late November 2016 after a heart attack in Hawaii, Honor and Cami took turns walking me to help me regain strength. I thought Honor was in superb shape her entire life. One evening in February 2017 after my walks with Cami and Honor, I remarked to Celinda in a telephone conversation that Honor, who was fourteen years and three months old at the time, would probably live until she was seventeen. As soon as I hung up the phone, though, I looked over and watched Honor in great discomfort as she was experiencing a series of small strokes that soon made her unable to stand or walk without great difficulty. I had her put to sleep at the local veterinarian's office at 8:30 a.m. the next morning as she was left with no decent quality of life. We are responsible for these Samoyeds and have to assist them when it is time.

Honor reminded me that we are here for just a short while, and we don't know our expiration date. One moment we are alive and well, and within a second or two, we could be near our end point.

Honor took a stand against cats at an early age. Author's collection.

Chapter 14

Ending

I hope you enjoyed this collection of stories. After *Rex of White Way, The Blizzard King* was published, readers wanted a second book about Rex with additional pictures. That gave me a reason to put together this collection of short stories in booklet form. As Jeanne Nonhof once said to me, "If you have been breeding long enough you will see just about everything." So that others may learn of what affects our breed, I have included details of diseases and health concerns in the stories. To leave them out is a disservice. The lifespan of a Samoyed is still so brief compared to ours.

From the Kauzlarich, Osborn, and Druse donations, we now have new pictures of Rex and a huge start to Rex's Library. I still don't understand how Madelin's spirit could have been waiting for me. I think I understand why, but not how it is possible.

We mention that dogs are waiting for us at "The Rainbow Bridge," but we still wonder what happens to Samoyeds or any dogs after they leave their mortal lives. The ancients thought they accompanied humans into the afterlife by guarding the passageway. Perhaps. I am hopeful of meeting up someday with Ono, Rex, Riley, Seattle, General, Cricket, Honor and all my Samoyeds when my remaining time as a temporary voyager on earth has come to an end.

Enjoy your dogs, watch closely for their behaviors, and I encourage you to write down your own stories no matter how unbelievable they may seem. Years ago, Wilna Coulter, an important Sammy owner, breeder, mentor, and exhibitor for many decades, was collecting stories of Sammies and their unusual behaviors from around the world. In particular, she told me a few stories of what the Sammies would do during a full moon in the northern hemisphere. Sadly, to my knowledge none of this has been saved.

As this book was in the final stages of drafting, I ended up in the hospital with chest pains and a small heart attack in Honolulu, Hawaii, in November 2016 and received a heart stent. Dr. Luu was the cardiologist, and Dr. Ono was the doctor on duty checking on me for each of the three days I was on my back. I am thankful that Ono's curse is over and that I recovered to publish this book.

—Jim Cheskawich

Mason Sams at Treasure Island 1938. Courtesy of the Kauzlarich Collection.

Credits for Part I

Photography:

1. From the Rex of White Way Samoyed Memorial Library Collections:
    A. Jim and Marian Osborn collection
    B. Walt and Jan Kauzlarich collection
    C. Madelin Druse collection
2. Jim Cheskawich personal collection
3. Celinda Cheskawich personal collection
4. Heather Stevenson Kelly Collection
5. Mardee Ward Fanning Rex photos
6. Anne O'Neill and the Polar Route photo
7. Joan Luna Liebes and several Cami photos
8. Linda Martinson and Cynthia Fleenor for "Purple Girl" photos

References and Sources

Caro, Robert A. *Master of the Senate: The Years of Lyndon Johnson, Volume 3.* New York, New York: Vintage Books, April 2002. (Chapter Five)

Cheskawich, Jim. *The Story of Rex of White Way, The Blizzard King.* Woodland, Washington: Rex the Blizzard King Stories, LLC, 2012. (Introduction and Chapter One)

Cheskawich, Jim. *Vietnam 1971, Remembering The "101st" Then And Now.* Woodland, Washington: Rex the Blizzard King Stories, LLC. Printed in Canada by Friesens, November 2016. (Chapter One)

Fishback, Lee. *Training Lead Dogs.* Nunica, Michigan: Tun-Dra, 1979. (Chapter Five)

Fishback, Mel. *Organization for the Working Samoyed Newsletter, The Yapper.* Boonville, New York, New York: Judy Schirber Publisher, August 1972. (Chapter One)

Hays, Galeen. *Policewoman One: My 20 Years on the LAPD.* New York, New York: Villard Books, May 26, 1992. (Chapter One)

Krauss, Bob and Wanda Krauss. *The Complete Pedigree Book of American Champion Samoyeds, 1907-1971, Volumes 1 and 2.* Madison, Wisconsin: Trustees of the Goodrich Fund, Straus Printing Company, October 1975. (Chapter One)

Lydecker-Hayford, Beatrice. *Walking the Thin Veil.* Maitland, Florida: Xulon Press, September 10, 2014. (Introduction)

McCullough, David. *1776*. New York: Simon and Schuster, May 24, 2005. (Chapter Five)

O'Brien, Tim. *The Things They Carried*. Boston, Massachusetts: Houghton Mifflin, March 28, 1990. (Introduction)

Puxley, W. Lavallin. *Samoyeds*. London, England: Williams & Norgate Ltd., Second Edition 1947. (Introduction)

Lawrence, Vera. "Samoyed Column." *Western Kennel World (WKW)* Magazines. San Francisco, California: WKW Press, 1938. (Chapter One)

Ward, Bob and Dolly Ward. *The New Complete Samoyed*. New York, New York: Howell Book House, Second Edition 1986. (Chapter One)

The Samoyed Quarterly Magazine. Arvada, Colorado: Hoflin Publishing Company, 1977-2011. (Chapter One and Four)

The Samoyed Club of America Bulletin. Jefferson City, Missouri; Woodland, Washington; and Cassleberry, Florida: Samoyed Club of America , 1945-2011. (Chapter One and Four)

Acknowledgements

I thank all of those I have met in the dog show world as judges, breeders, exhibitors, stewards, SCA members, or observers. I thank the "ancients" who preserved this breed through careful breedings and for recording Samoyed history so someone like me could come along and enjoy the research and develop multiple offshoot projects such as the Rex Library and now several books. Agnes Mason, Bob Ward, and Helen Harris were a huge inspiration for me as SCA president, exhibitor, breeder, and now as an historian entrusted with protecting and preserving the breed. Many doors truly opened for me as I wore different hats in the dog show world. I learned something from each of you and continue to learn new things about this marvelous breed every day! I am especially grateful to the Rex of White Way Samoyed Memorial Library and Museum for allowing me to use archival pictures donated by Jim and Marian Osborn, Walt and Jan Kauzlarich, and Madelin Druse. I thank Annie Reid and Cheryl Lynn West for joining me in producing this Trilogy Collection and for Lynne Holsapple and Kristie Kempker for editing, formatting, and designing the final layout. This was another project that never seemed like work and moved along easily.

Jim Cheskawich 11/13/2017

Part II
EVER AFTER

A Love Story

By Anngharaad "Annie" Reid

*Photo of Jamie, UKC Ch. Archaeus Irresistible for Smiliesam
Photo by the Author, Annie Reid.*

*Unless otherwise noted, all of the charcoal drawings and
handmade art pieces depicted within are the
artwork of the author, Annie Reid.*

To Girls and the Dogs that Love Them

Faith is believing in things you don't understand.
Hope is the conviction of things not seen.
Intuition is the power to know something without proof or evidence.
Knowledge is the state of becoming aware.
Revelation is the act of communicating truth.

Prayers can be demonstrative, raucous, and communal,
involving the use of words, hymns, or incantations made on bended knee;
more often, however, they are the silent wishes, the desperate hopes,
and the heartfelt desires made when we are at our most vulnerable,
our most disheartened, and our most inconsolable.

Prologue

Niki
My Angel of Destiny

(May 28, 1968–August 12, 1982)

> Sleeping softly, then it seems
> Heaven enters in my dreams;
> Angels hover round me,
> Whisp'ring they have found me;
> Two are sweetly singing,
> Two are garlands bringing,
> Strewing me with roses
> As my soul reposes.
> God will not forsake me
> When dawn at last will wake me.
>
> (Engelbert Humperdinck and Adelheid Wette, *Hänsel & Gretel*)

One September night when I was twelve years old, my grandmother—against my father's "over my dead body" protestations and to my subsequent delight—kidnapped my cousin's Samoyed puppy, secured her the following morning to a maple tree under my bedroom window, and woke me. To this day I can close my eyes, smell the crispness of that September morning, see the spray of sunlight splash across her smiling, upturned face, and feel my heart explode with joy.

Four months earlier my older sister's Samoyed had given birth to a litter of five puppies, and I had claimed her, the only female, when she was just three days old. I had taken advantage of every opportunity that summer to play with her and had tried, without any success, to convince my parents to let me keep her. It was out of the question as we already owned a cat and a dog. I admit to being more than a little angry when my sister gave my puppy to my cousin. I admit to being more than a little horrified when I learned that my cousin was relocating to a facility that couldn't accept dogs and was encouraged to euthanize her. Thank goodness my grandmother interceded. She that once was lost to me was now found, and I could not believe my good fortune when my mother decided that it would be too cruel to separate us again. I think my mother wanted her, too. She had fallen in love with this breed after rescuing her Samoyed, Boy, when she was just twenty-two years of age. He had died shortly before I was born, but his adventures became family folklore. It was not surprising that Boy would start a family tradition of Samoyed ownership.

Boy, 1938-1953
(Photo from the private collection of the author, Annie Reid)

And so it came to pass that Niki became my foundation Samoyed and my ticket to a lifelong promise of happiness, love, and loyalty. She made me a better human being. Because the simplicity of her love was so genuine and beautiful, she, more than any relative, teacher, clergyman, or human friend, taught me that love is kind, love has no boundaries, and love is enduring. Niki slept beside my bed, listened without judgment to all my complaints, waited patiently at the window for me to come home from school, rested her head on my foot whenever I practiced the piano, kept me company while I did my homework, licked hundreds of tears from my face, and forgave me for going away to college. Fourteen years later, my father and I, with tears in our eyes that she couldn't lick away, buried her remains under her maple tree.

I then left my home and ran away from all the memories of her that it held.

Memories are curious little demons. Perhaps I didn't want to manage them; perhaps I encouraged them to become confrontational and interrupt my thoughts. I was so lonely without her, and the memories kept her close. At first they fixated on the details of her death, but in time, they were replaced with a warm appreciation of her life.

This is my tribute to Niki. This is my love story to her and to all my amazing Samoyeds that continued her legacy. Because of them, I always trust my intuition, I always believe in things I can't explain, I always dare to hope, and I no longer say goodbye.

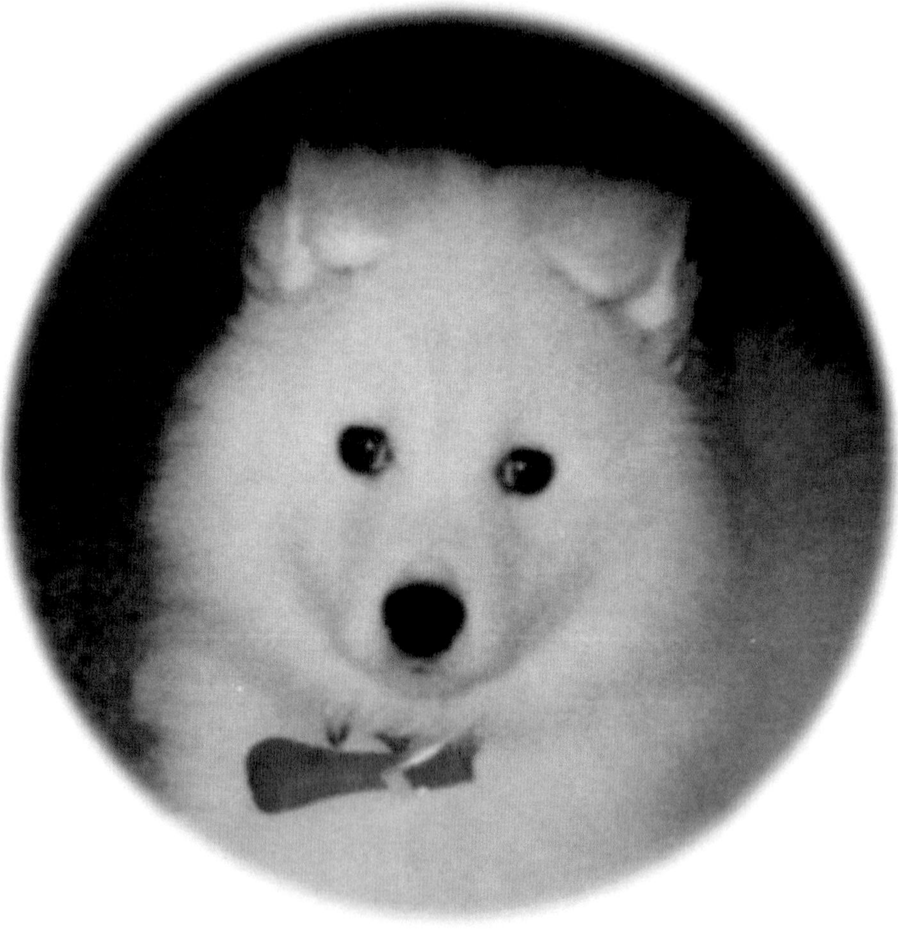

Beau
My Angel of Enlightenment

(December 22, 1982–June 25, 1998)

> "Be with me always—take any form—drive me mad!
> only *do* not leave me in this abyss, where I cannot find you!
> Oh, God! it is unutterable!
> I *cannot* live without my life!
> I *cannot* live without my soul!"
>
> (Emily Brontë, *Wuthering Heights*)

If I had ever entertained the belief that I exercised free will, that belief was shattered on February 19, 1983. On that morning my intention was to go to the mall and buy lipstick. Instead, I took a wrong turn, kept walking toward what I thought was my intended destination, and eventually found myself before the mall's pet store. I hesitated to enter. I was prepared for a puppy; I had lost my Niki six months previously and knew that the only way to honor her was to find another animal companion, another Samoyed. I had gone so far as to reserve a female Samoyed puppy from an upcoming litter. But then I found myself at what I thought was the wrong place at the wrong time, but there he was waiting for me.

He was the last of the Samoyed puppies to be adopted. According to the clerk, he showed little interest in any of the other potential adoptees, and the clerk apologized in advance for what would surely be a disappointing introduction. I dismissed her concern as I wasn't interested in a male. At my insistence, because I selfishly wanted to satisfy a badly needed puppy "fix," she reluctantly took him out of his crate and placed him in my arms.

That's all it took. What that clerk put together, no man could put asunder.

Puppy Beau
(Photo by the author, Annie Reid)

I named him Beau, and for many years the two of us enjoyed each other's company in serene contentment. I loved him so. He was my first thought every morning and my last thought at night. We were inseparable, and although I could never—for fear of ridicule—put the feeling into words, I couldn't resist the notion that I knew him from a previous life experience. There was something undeniably special about his quiet and affectionate protectiveness of me. Was our chance meeting at the mall actually a predetermined event? Or was it just a happy circumstance? I held these questions in my heart and reflected upon them often.

As years passed, my happiness was increasingly interrupted by the unbearable knowledge that one day Beau would be taken from me; Beau's happiness was more immediately interrupted by the boyfriend factor. Only *I* would fall instantly and completely in love with a man who wooed me with dog treats, and Ron wisely knew that his future with me depended upon how well he and Beau got along. Although Beau accepted Ron into our household, he did so reluctantly. To his credit, Ron never missed an opportunity to spoil Beau, demonstrate sincere affection for him, or spare any expense to keep him comfortable as he aged.

*Ron and Beau
(Photo by the author, Annie Reid)*

*Official wedding photo, December 26, 1992
(Photo by Jeff Reid, used with permission)*

Although Ron loved Beau, I wouldn't describe the affection he felt toward him as passionate. Sadly, none of my employers and few of my acquaintances were pet enthusiasts. Most were parents who understandably concentrated their attentions on their children. I was, therefore, delighted when, on a whim, I attended a presentation on animal communication and found myself among enlightened, like-minded individuals who held as their basic tenet a reverence for all living creatures and who renounced the patronizing attitude that animals are less intelligent. I was overjoyed and overwhelmed to hear personal testimony proving the phenomenon of animal reincarnation. Excited, I enrolled Beau and myself in an interactive weekend workshop where I hoped to develop animal communications skills that I could put into practice.

The workshop was a three-day event hosted by a couple in western Connecticut. Friday evening's session was a textbook presentation on the method and science of animal communication. Animals, the lecturer instructed, communicate with us telepathically, and their voices vary. They speak to us by using words, sending visual images, or expressing emotion. Animals in spirit also use dreams as a communication medium. Whatever voice or medium they choose to use, their messages are always communicated with love, eloquence, and sincerity. As an added bonus, the lecturer included insight into animal reincarnation and asserted that animals, unlike humans, had perfect recollections of their past lives. I hoped the workshop wouldn't prove disappointing.

On the second day, as snow fell outside, twelve students and nine dogs gathered together in a warm, dimly lit, cozily furnished room and sat in a circle around the instructor. While some students chose to sit on the blanket-draped upholstered sofas and chairs, I made the fortuitous decision to sit on the floor beside Beau and next to Kathi and her Collie, Caleb. Here, in this comfortable and peaceful setting, we practiced meditation exercises to cleanse our minds and free them to recognize and trust our intuitions. If animal communication is telepathic and intuitive, then only after we learn to recognize and trust our intuitive capabilities can we communicate telepathically. We practiced on each other first, before breaking out into groups to practice on each other's animal companions.

To my delight, Beau proved to be an excellent communicator and quickly became a favorite study subject. At the end of the second day, we were assigned to an animal companion other than our own and instructed to ask about past lives. I don't recall if I had any success, but Kathi, one of the other students, as well as the instructor hit the jackpot when all three spoke with Beau, and all three received the same amazing message.

Beau spoke in words, images, and emotions. He showed each communicator a young couple walking with arms linked over a lamp-lit, cobblestoned bridge. The man was dressed in formal attire. The woman was dark-haired and dressed in a full-length, red-sequined gown. They were lovers on their way to an event, possibly a dance.

Beau then showed each communicator the image of a vintage military aircraft spiraling downward, leaving a billow of smoke in its wake.

From the images Beau presented, each communicator deduced that these events took place overseas—perhaps and most probably in Great Britain during World War II.

Then the instructor took me aside. She wanted to relay the rest of Beau's communication to me privately. It broke my heart to learn that he was sad and frustrated by the physical limitations of his canine body, and it concerned me to learn that he feared I would do something foolish upon his death. The latter was his greatest worry. I would have to choose the words I used to express my affection for him more carefully, but first I had to find the man behind the dog.

The rest of the workshop was, for me, anticlimactic. It concluded on Sunday with exercises using telepathy to gain access into the body to detect pain or illness. Before we left, Kathi and I exchanged email addresses with a promise to practice our newly learned skills on each other's companions. It was a promise we kept, and I am so glad of it. We couldn't have known it then, but we would become each other's lifelines after she lost her Caleb and I lost my Beau. After all these years, we are still close. I wonder, was it my choice to sit next to Kathi? Or was it Beau's and Caleb's?

The following Monday I went to the local public library and perused the World War II reference section, specifically books about the Royal Air Force. I randomly pulled out a volume and its pages automatically opened to a section describing the Bristol Beaufighter. Known simply as the "Beau," the Beaufighter was a twin-engine aircraft developed by the United Kingdom's Bristol Aeroplane Company, introduced in July 1939, and deployed by the Royal Air Force during the height of the Battle of Britain. It was humbling to admit that he, not I, chose his name. In my research I also found a listing of all the names of those brave young souls lost during the Battle of Britain, their Squadron Numbers, their dates of death, and the planes flown. It was a start.

That evening, sitting cross-legged next to Beau, I held that book with its listing of all those names on my lap. I asked him to bark when he heard his. Ron thought this was pure silliness and frequently teased me with a few barks of his own. (A few glaring looks of mine put an end to that nonsense.) It took awhile, but when I called out the name of a certain air gunnery sergeant, he responded with two whimpers and a bark. I continued reading the names, but he didn't utter another sound. I looked up the air gunnery sergeant's statistics and amazingly discovered that he was posted to the 219 Squadron and was killed on September 30, 1940, when his aircraft disintegrated and crashed during a routine patrol. Smoke was reported in the aircraft prior to the crash. Was it a coincidence that I found Beau on February 19 (2-19)?

How many times have I turned to God and thanked him for all of my guardian angels. First there was Niki. Then there was Beau. Ron may have been my third angel, but he would never be my least. I thank God that Ron was there to comfort me on the evening of June 25, 1998, when my darling Beau bloated for the second time in three days. I asked for and found the courage to make the unselfish decision to offer him a peaceful passing. My dearest friend and his veterinarian, Dr. Margaret "Peggy" McIsaac, came to the house, administered a sedative, and drove an hour to her clinic and back again so that he could pass in my arms and in the presence of all those who held him dear. At 3:00 a.m., as I was massaging his velvety ears and kissing his paws for the last time, he broke my heart, but not before I could whisper in those velvety ears a final request. I asked him not to leave me in the dark to finish my journey without him. I asked him to return. I told him that I would light an electric candle in an upstairs window to help guide his way home; the bulb would burn out when he no longer needed its light.

The following morning, Ron and I buried him in the backyard. Afterwards, Ron turned to me and asked me to promise him that I would not do anything foolish, that I would not leave him to finish this journey alone. Stunned, I asked him to repeat what he had just asked, but he couldn't. He couldn't because it was Beau, not Ron, talking to me. Beau heard me, and I heard him. How often had I told Beau that I couldn't and wouldn't live without him? No, I promised Beau, although I longed to be where he was, I won't harm myself. I won't take my life.

Why are we humans so afraid to show our vulnerability? Why do we wait until tragedy strikes before we dare to display observable expressions of emotion? I came home from Mass the following Sunday to find Ron on the living room sofa crying. We were both in such exquisite grief. We did what we could to console each other, but he could think of only one solution, and he acted upon that impulse and contacted the Minuteman Samoyed Club. I contacted my animal communication instructor and arranged a consult. I also left a message for Kathi.

To apply for membership in the Minuteman Samoyed Club, one must be sponsored by two club members, attend three club events, and currently own a Samoyed. We began our initiation by attending a club-sponsored herding event, where Ron met a breeder who shared with us his happy news of a litter of five Samoyed puppies "on the ground." These puppies were born on August 17, 1998.

If I looked forward to attending these club events with eagerness, I looked forward to the consultation with my animal communication instructor with apprehension. It is possible to contact an animal in spirit, and I was anxious to know how Beau would respond to my questions. Would he reincarnate and return to me? If so, how would I recognize him? I knew who Beau was in my prior lifetime, but I was curious to know if we had met before in my current lifetime.

My instructor assured me that Beau would return. He—as all creatures can—would manipulate events to guarantee a successful outcome or reunion; all I had to do was trust and have patience that everything would happen according to plan and that the timing, opportunity, and outcome would be perfect. I would recognize him by his eyes: the shape, the depth, the pools, the promise of understanding, the reflection of the love visible within. He would return in the winter, as a gift from Ron.

Beau revealed that he and I had been together in many lifetimes. My instructor explained that soul mates reincarnate simultaneously. If the life of one of the "mates" ends tragically or prematurely, it is possible for that soul to return as a species with a shorter lifespan in order to maintain the harmonious cycle of death and rebirth. Theoretically, if Beau, Ron, and I are soul mates and share this lifetime, we each must have died during the 1940s. I often speculate if Ron was one of the two other crewmen—either the pilot or the radar operator—killed when that ill-fated aircraft disintegrated and crashed on September 30, 1940. I believe that I died by my own hand, a casualty of heartache and despair. In this, my current lifetime, Beau was a childhood friend of mine, a playmate who died tragically while still a teenager. I had cared very much for this boy who lived in our neighborhood. We grew up together. He was just nineteen years of age when his life ended in a fatal car crash in September 1976. I was being tested. This time, I needed to look to Ron, my other soul mate, for strength. This time, I needed to reach beyond myself. I needed to find the courage to believe that Beau and I would be reunited. I needed to rejoice in and choose life.

One Saturday, Ron took me out to dinner at the Macaroni Grill where wait staff serenade the diners. I waited, but none of the singers approached our table. Just as Ron was paying the bill, one of the waiters came over and asked if he could sing to me, in Italian, one of his favorite love songs. I imagined it was Beau singing to me. As soon as he finished, one of the waitresses approached us and began to sing "You'll Never Walk Alone."

I walked out of that restaurant holding my head high because I had hope in my heart, and I knew I wasn't walking alone.

Cornelia
My Angel of Compassion

(August 17, 1998–July 14, 2013)

> Billow and breeze, islands and seas,
> Mountains of rain and sun,
> All that was good, all that was fair,
> All that was me is gone.

(Robert Louis Stevenson, "Sing me a Song of a Lad that is Gone")

Beau would be a hard act to follow. But follow him she did. Cornelia was one of the litter of puppies Ron had learned about at the Minuteman Samoyed Club herding event. Born on August 17, 1998, Cornelia came into our lives on October 13, 1998. Effervescent, bubbly, joyful—she was my bottle of champagne, my caviar dreams, my winning lottery ticket, my prize in a box of Cracker Jack. In the banquet that was her life, she didn't starve, and she wouldn't allow me to either. We took on so many challenges together, and I think we faced them brilliantly. Not to offend St. Paul, but it was Cornelia that taught me the purest form of love: it is patient, it is kind, it does not envy, it does not dishonor others, it is not self-seeking, it is not easily angered, it keeps no record of wrongs. It always protects, always trusts, always hopes, always perseveres. It never fails. (1 Cor. 13:4-8 New International Version)

We nicknamed her "Corny," and we celebrated her homecoming by throwing her a party. We invited our neighbors, our relatives, and our friends; we served "chili-con-Corny," corndogs, cornbread, popcorn, corn chips, and, for desert, "Sam-ores." I would give anything for the chance to be at that party again, to hold that darling puppy in my arms one more time, and to tell her how much I loved and appreciated her and how much I miss her. She was my salvation. She was the star I wished upon, a balm for my aching heart, a tonic. We doted on her, and although she loved both Ron and me, I would always be the focus of her attentions and worry.

Our first night together: setting up her playpen
(Photo by Ron Reid, used with permission)

I cherish my memories of her first Christmas and New Year's Eve. How tolerant she was when I put her in an old steamer trunk with rolls of wrapping paper, threw ribbons over her head, and forced her to sit still as I took Christmas card photos. On numerous occasions I ran after her as she snatched and grabbed a Christmas candle light off of a windowsill. I hung a pink silk stocking decorated with lace and antique braidings from the mantle, in between Ron's and mine, and filled it with toys and treats. We both rushed home from a holiday party to be with her as we welcomed in the New Year. Happy days were here again.

Corny's first Christmas card photo
(Photo by the author, Annie Reid)

Ron and I had always planned on having two Samoyeds in our household, and we hoped for a male puppy out of a litter due to whelp in mid-March. On March 15, 1999, Corny dug a hole in the snow covering Beau's grave. Ron was convinced that this was a sign. At 11:15 p.m. that evening, our Tristan was born. Although Corny's kingdom would soon be invaded by a Samoyed puppy, her status as queen of my heart would never be challenged.

For most of her life, Corny was one of two animal companions in our household. For many years, I devoted much time and energy on Tristan's show career. Although I focused on her wants and needs with the same ferocity that I devoted to Tristan's training and celebrity, I always felt guilty. If she harbored any resentment, she never showed it. She would wait patiently at home whenever I took him to class or a dog show. Her love was patient, her love was kind, it did not envy. It kept no record of wrongs.

If she had a fault, it was thievery and extortion. She was master of the "snatch and grab," and under the bed was where she would often run with her loot. Anything not bolted down was fair game: shoes, loaded paint brushes, towels, golf gloves, socks, and hair brushes to name a few examples. She would hold her prize hostage until I paid the appropriate ransom. I don't know how she knew, but she understood the value of each item. I had to pay more in dog treats for a valuable item, such as a shoe, and less for an invaluable item, such as a towel. This could actually be added to her list of virtues.

Corny holding a blanket hostage
(Photo by the author, Annie Reid)

Corny was always stoic. For most of her life she was plagued with sore knees following an injury sustained running to Tristan's aid when two neighborhood dogs tried to breach our fence to attack him. I heard Corny squeal, I turned to see the two aggressive dogs, and I spotted their clueless owner skipping towards our property. I went berserk. I called Tristan to me, picked up Corny, and, as I held her in my arms, shouted several colorful expletives at the owner. Dr. Peggy McIsaac diagnosed a ruptured cruciate ligament.

Her stoicism failed her after Tristan's death. Fearing she would fall into his freshly dug grave, Ron insisted that she be confined a few yards away as we buried him. That was a mistake—her howls and cries were heartbreaking. Rather than falling into his grave, she fell into depression. She missed him; we all did. But just as Clarence Oddbody knew that he could save George Bailey by jumping into the river, Corny knew that if she challenged me to minister to her needs, I would heal. A million bells could ring, but they would never create an angel like my Corny. Her love always protected.

Me and my darling Corny-Girl
(Photo by Lynne Graves, used with permission)

Not to boast, but I am rather good at pet portraiture and have drawn several nice portraits of Beau, Corny, and Tristan. The act of using my hands has always been therapeutic for me, and I itched to channel my grief artistically. At Ron's insistence I enrolled in classes at a local art studio. My teacher, Barbara, encouraged me to explore other artistic avenues and expand my appreciation for different mediums. Under Barbara's tutelage I created paper-maché and glass sculptures of Corny and Tristan, painted cardboard houses depicting them in the front windows, distressed shaker boxes and stenciled their silhouettes on the lids, and decorated candle jars with paint, glitter, and their photos. As I created my little masterpieces, Corny lay in her favorite spot under the piano and kept me company. I credit both Corny and Tristan for introducing me to the world of high-end crafting and to the very talented Barbara, whom I hold close to my heart and consider the dearest of friends. Many of my little creations have been duplicated to help others manage grief. Art, in all its forms, is the universal language of the heart.

Paper-maché and glass sculptures of Tristan and Corny

Corny and Tristan's silhouettes on distressed Shaker boxes

Painted cardboard house

Candle jars

And so we carried on. Over the next two years I redirected all my stress and worry onto Corny and her arthritic knees. We went to an acupuncturist monthly to help her manage her pain, and she thrived. Other than her knees, she was in amazing health.

In the meantime we anxiously awaited the birth and arrival of our new Samoyed, Jamie. I anguished over the decision to introduce a puppy into a household with a veteran. But I knew that if this was Tristan returning to me, I couldn't question the timing or deny the opportunity.

Jamie proved to be a blessing. He revived Corny and reawakened her dormant maternal instincts. She taught him manners, and he respected her status as head of household.

Corny was almost fifteen years of age when we celebrated Jamie's first birthday on June 3, 2013. Her health declined quickly thereafter, and I agonized over the inevitable. On the morning of July 14, 2013, a Sunday morning, she made the decision easy for me. I found her under our bed listless but still alive.

Somehow I got her out from under the bed and called Dr. McIsaac. Peggy arrived at my house at approximately 1:00 in the afternoon. She recognized the expression of relief and appreciation on Corny's face. It's an expression she has witnessed several times. It was the granting of permission.

With just a little help from me, Corny stubbornly walked on all four legs down the ramp Ron had built for her and into the backyard. Peggy and I sat under another maple tree, and as I held Corny in my lap with my arms around her, I celebrated her life while Jamie ran about. When it was "time," my darling little Corny-girl passed peacefully in my loving embrace, taking so much that was good and fair from me. She taught me that it is okay to be human; she loved me in spite of that and forgave me for all my shortcomings. Her love never failed.

Was she my Niki? I suspect that she was. When she was just a puppy, Kathi asked Corny if there was anything important she wished to tell me. Her simple response expressed regret at "not being able to save me the last time" and happiness at "being here now." Although I asked her to return to me, I knew I didn't need to. She told me her new name. For some time I contemplated calling my next female Samoyed "Geillis"—or "Geilie" for short—after the suspected witch in Diana Gabaldon's *Outlander* novels. I thought the shortened form of the name charming but hesitated to brand a puppy a "witch." When I finally chose to do so, just a few days before Corny's passing, I knew that Corny had given me her consent.

Me and my darling Cornelia
(Drawing by the author, Annie Reid, from a photograph by Lynne Graves)

Farewell my little star, my lass that was now gone. Each morning I awoke and knew that I was one day closer to seeing her again. Each morning I woke and called her home. Each morning I awoke and shouted to the Heavens, "Hurry home, Geilie."

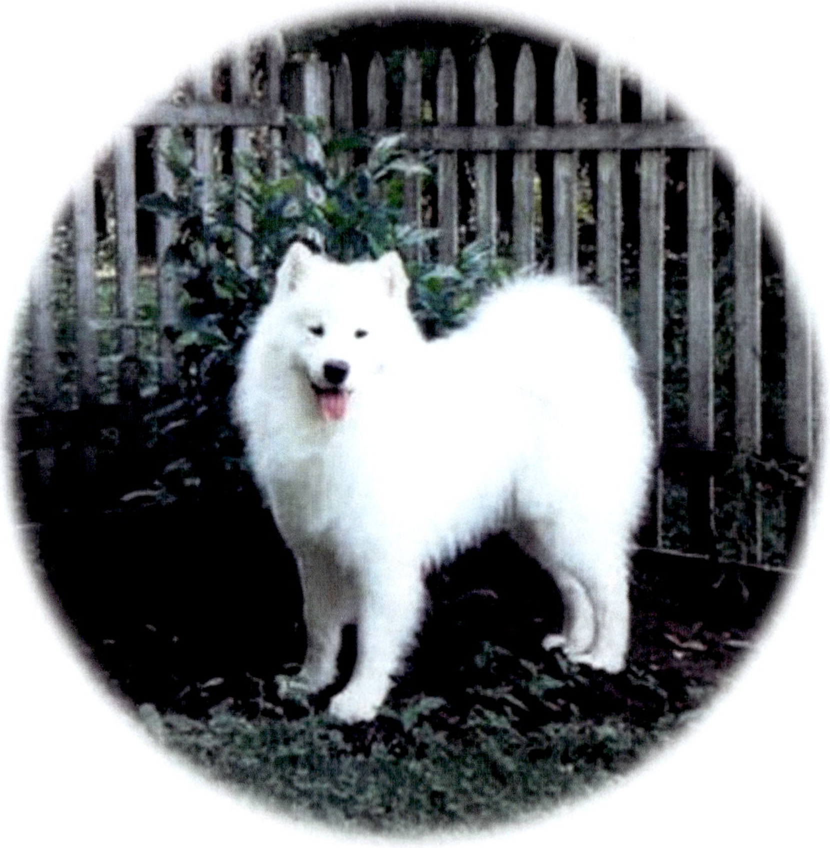

Tristan
The Angel of My Heart

(March 15, 1999–April 7, 2010)

> "When he shall die,
> Take him and cut him out in little stars,
> And he will make the face of heaven so fine
> That all the world will be in love with night
> And pay no worship to the garish sun."
>
> (William Shakespeare, *Romeo and Juliet*)

There is a macabre comfort in the act of grieving; clinging to memories and allowing them to swaddle you in their warmth is consoling. I am a master at it. But I knew if I wanted Beau's spirit to return, I had to surrender it to the universe; I had to return him to the Heavens; I had to let him fly home, if only for a while. I had to give him time to manipulate events to guarantee our reunion.

And manipulate events he did. I recognized each and every one of his prophetically significant clues; I danced to his carefully choreographed steps. Tristan was given to me without my asking. I found him without my seeking. The door to my soul was opened without my knocking. He was my found treasure.

My beloved Tristan
(Photo by Lynn Graves, used with permission)

During the summer of 1998, I met several Samoyed breeders. One had a particularly special bond with her male, and I hoped for one of his puppies. Unfortunately, she was not considering breeding him at that time. That was disappointing news, but I remembered Beau's instructions to trust and be patient, his prophesy that our reunion would happen according to plan, and his prediction that the outcome would be perfect.

There were times when it was difficult to remain trusting and patient. Beau's choreography would test my faith by leading me into and through the valley of despair. I went to sleep every night clutching Beau's favorite plush toy to my heart hoping for a message in my dreams. None were received. Kathi and I practiced communicating with our companions in spirit. I practiced on Caleb and she, Beau. We could contact their spirits until such time as they began their return. I anxiously waited for the day Kathi could no longer reach Beau. I could only hope that the promise of Beau's words would sustain me.

Summer was coming to an end, and my birthday was approaching. I was dreading it. For years my mother would wrap up a gift for me from Beau. These were just little trinkets, but I always looked forward to receiving them. It saddened me to know that there wouldn't be any such remembrance this year. Ron tried to help. He would foolishly ask me what I wanted, and I would repeatedly and hopelessly respond "Beau." We made the decision to swap birthdays. We would celebrate his in September and mine in December. Corny was my gift to Ron and my boy, whenever he arrived, would be Ron's gift to me. In the end, all this dread, sadness, and rearranging was unnecessary. On September 27, 1998, the anniversary of my birth, my one wish, my desperate desire was heard and granted. Beau did remember me with a gift. It was wrapped up in a much anticipated email message from Kathi. She wrote: "I believe that Beau has started the return. Good luck . . . Godspeed, my friend."

All I had to do now was wait and experience events as they unfolded. On January 4, 1999, the Samoyed breeder I had met the previous summer sent me an email message telling me that she had decided to breed her male to her female in about two weeks. That meant puppies in March. On March 8, 1999, the bulb in the candle I left burning in the upstairs window to guide Beau home burnt out. On March 15, 1999, Corny dug a hole in the snow covering Beau's grave. The next morning, as I sat at my desk working, I received an email which read: "Hi. Your BOY was born at 11:15 last night." As it was prophesied, so it happened. He was born in winter, and he would be a gift from Ron.

The night before Ron and I were to meet Tristan for the first time, I dreamt that there were black and brown puppies, as well as Samoyed puppies, at the breeder's house. I would soon learn that this was Beau's way of letting me know, beyond a shadow of any doubt, that my search was over. I found Tristan waiting for me in a whelping box next to a litter of Welsh Terrier puppies. My treasure was found. And forever thereafter, wherever he was, there also was my heart.

Puppy Tristan
(Photo by the author, Annie Reid)

Every time I beheld him, he took my breath away. Every time I think about him, I have to catch my breath. He was my Tristan, and I was his Iseult; we treasured each other with the same intoxicating intensity. Our love was blessed by the angels and preserved from extinction by great devotion.

Me and my Tristan
(Photo by Lynn Graves, used with permission)

Many years of grass now cover his grave, but he does not rest there quietly. He haunts me. I can stand ringside at a dog show and recall with perfect clarity how beautifully he showed for and with me. If I lie down on the sofa and close my eyes, I can still feel him jump up and gingerly creep into the narrow crevice between my body and the cushions, lay his head on my chest, and fall asleep. I recall with fondness how he would get my attention by mashing his muzzle against my thigh. And I recall with bewilderment how, whenever he was sick to his stomach, he would jump up, put his paws around my waist or shoulder and hold me close. To this day I recall how angry I was to learn from Ron that—on the days preceding his final day of life—he cried for hours at the window after I left for work. I hold back tears recalling his last day of life. I wonder where I found the strength to carry him like a toddler into the house for the last time, his hind legs wrapped around my waist, his front paws around my neck, and his head resting on my shoulder.

Tristan with a favorite toy
(Photo by the author, Annie Reid)

Tristan
(Photo by Lynn Graves, used with permission)

I said good night to my beloved, brave, lovely, and unforgettable boy on April 7, 2010, believing with absolute certainty that our souls are pledged for eternity and can never be parted, not even in death. Just as the intertwining vine and rose tree growing from the graves of the legendary Tristan and Iseult symbolized their undying love, so, too, do the tethers connecting our souls. No matter how many times our vines are cut, I know they will join again.

Me and my beloved Tristan
(Drawing by the author, Annie Reid, from a photograph by Lynne Graves)

But now his vine needed reseeding. Where would I plant it? I listened to my quiet little voice. I wagered all my hopes and dreams. I took a chance. On June 5, 2010, I contacted Hazel, a friend and breeder in Derbyshire, England, who, not so coincidentally, had met Tristan and Corny at the 2007 Samoyed Club of America National Specialty. I asked if she would consider offering me a puppy from her next breeding. The seed was planted the instant she said "yes."

I would call my little seedling Jamie. To the rest of the world he is UKC Ch. Archaeus Irresistible for Smiliesam, or Mr. Irresistible.

Jamie

The Angel of All My Dreams Come True

(June 3, 2012–Present)

"Whatever our souls are made of,
his and mine are the same…"

(Emily Brontë, *Wuthering Heights*)

As Londoners celebrated Queen Elizabeth II's Diamond Jubilee, Ron and I celebrated Jamie's birth. We continue to rejoice in our good fortune—every day with him is a holiday, a treat. If Beau was a bowl of ice cream and Tristan whipped cream, Jamie is the cherry on top.

He is the product of a very collaborative and careful breeding effort. His dam, Sunni, was bred from old and respected English, Finnish, Danish, and Czechoslovakian bloodlines. His sire, Flymo, was bred from old and respected English, Finnish, Danish, Czechoslovakian, and Australian bloodlines. Both of his parents are co-owned and co-loved by his co-breeders, Hazel and Penny. We were told to expect a male with a broad back skull, a soft muzzle, small ears, and a big mane. What an understatement. Jamie is not only the most breathtakingly beautiful Samoyed I have ever laid eyes upon, but he is also the most charming. He is sensitive, gentle, patient, smart, and loving. He is, in a word, irresistible.

UKC Ch. Archaeus Irresistible for Smiliesam
(Photo by Katie Rogers, Smiling Wolf Photography, used with permission)

Attention readers, please indulge me,
As I reveal how David and Penny,
In two thousand twelve, on the third of June,
As Londoners rejoiced that afternoon,
Helped Sunni whelp her puppies three.

An ultrasound had confirmed that Sunni's breeding to Flymo was successful, and Sunni was due to whelp her puppies on or about June 3, 2012. Ultrasounds, unfortunately, cannot confirm with certainty the number of live births or reveal each puppy's sex. Ron and I had wept and prayed when Hazel emailed us the ultrasound results. We wept and prayed again when she emailed us news that Sunni had whelped her first puppy—a boy. Another boy and a girl followed. It was a happy day for us, for a family in England, and for a family in Spain.

Jamie and his siblings were born outside of London at Penny's house. When they were just three days old, Penny's husband, David, installed a Puppy Cam over the whelping box and linked it to her Facebook feed. It was a brilliant idea. Sunni

Archaeus Irresistible for Smiliesam—Jamie
(Photo by the author, Annie Reid)

Ice Maiden Smile Yoshi and us—Sunni
(Jamie's Dam)

Smiliesam Skirt Chaser—Flymo
(Jamie's Sire)

Smiliesam Shikira—Kiki
(Sunni's Dam)

FCI Int Ch Benji of Xamba Yoshi and us—Benji (Sunni's Sire)

JCh, UK Ch Absolute Xamba Yoshi & us—Azi
(Flymo's Dam)

Aust Ch, UK Ch Snerzok Strike Chaser—Chase
(Flymo's Sire)

(Photos courtesy of Hazel Fitzgibbon, Jana Fulierová, Michele O'Brien, and Penny Roberts; used with permission)

and her puppies became Facebook reality stars as Ron and I and hundreds of our "friends" watched with fascination as the little seedlings grew and prospered.

> *David said to his wife, "In a few days*
> *Once the newborns pass that critical phase,*
> *And we have had a chance to relax,*
> *Over the whelping box I can attach,*
> *A camera to serve as an 'eye'*
> *For those on Facebook to watch and spy*
> *On the puppies and to let it be shown*
> *To all our friends from the comfort of our home*
> *How well the puppies have grown."*

Sunni and her fourteen-day-old Flymo puppies
(Photo by Penny Roberts, used with permission)

We witnessed—fascinated—the insane and yet adorable stages of puppyhood: the vulnerability and dependence upon Momma, the eating and sleeping, the round bellies, the opening of eyes and ears, the wobbly attempts at walking and ear piercing attempts at vocalization, the emergence of razor sharp teeth through pink gums, puppy play, and their growing awareness of humans and other dogs. In short, we watched their personalities develop. As they did, Ron and I would speculate about which boy was ours.

We had already decided to call our boy "Jamie" after James Fraser, the swashbuckling hero of Diana Gabaldon's *Outlander* novels. Choosing his Kennel Club registered name would, however, prove challenging. Penny, Hazel, and I finally settled on Archaeus (Penny's kennel name) Irresistible for Smiliesam (Hazel's kennel name). But which of two boys would I call Jamie the Irresistible? That decision was settled when he was just six weeks old. After evaluating the puppies, Hazel and Penny chose Boy #2 for us and announced their decision to us via email:

"Hello, my name is Jamie, and I am irresistible."
(Photo by Penny Roberts, used with permission)

Each morning with a flick of a switch,
We would wake and watch the puppies, transfixed,
As they opened their ears and their eyes,
Ron and I watched them, mesmerized.
Which boy was ours? We would speculate.
For six weeks we would watch and wait,
'til Penny attached to an email
A photo most adorable
Of Jamie the Irresistible.

Wretched are those who doubt and worry, for they shall become anxious. Prophetically reassuring dreams and clues eluded me. Is Jamie irresistible? Are our souls tethered? Would the pet relocation company Hazel recommended safely transport him from Heathrow to New Jersey? I had to relinquish any illusion of control and trust that they were and that they would.

Jamie
(Drawing by the author, Annie Reid,
from a photograph by Penny Roberts)

Jamie could travel as soon as he was eleven weeks old, and the next few weeks would be eventful ones for the puppies and their people. They enjoyed playtime in the garden, survived the indignity of baths, endured car rides, passed their veterinarian and eye checks with flying colors, received all their "jabs," and were microchipped. When they were eight weeks old he and his sister, Mitzi, said goodbye to their brother, Hugo, who went to live with his new family in Norfolk, Great Britain.

Hugo, Jamie, and Mitzi-Moo at eight weeks of age
(Photo by Penny Roberts, used with permission)

The weeks passed by, and I would ponder
Soon their world would be torn asunder.
In August there's a knock at the door,
And eavesdropping pups listened with glee
At the cries of a young family
Running towards them with arms opened wide.
But sadness would triumph when from the floor
Hugo would be picked from among the three
To live in the English countryside.

Hugo and Jamie
(Drawing by the author, Annie Reid, from a photograph by Penny Roberts)

I often wonder how Sunni felt seeing her little ones leave, and I wish I could tell her what Penny and Hazel already knew. I wish I could tell her that she could trust me to care for her little boy. I wish I could tell her that I would love him with all of my heart. He would want for nothing. He would never know cold or hunger or thirst. He would be my constant thought and worry. I would make his care and happiness my ultimate priority. I would love and treasure him always.

I needed to tell Jamie this, too. Penny described him as being incredibly sensitive, and I didn't want him to experience any anxiety as he left his family. I wanted to reassure him that he would be safe on the plane. I wanted him to know that I was waiting and waiting impatiently for him across the sea. And my new animal communicator—Cathy Malkin, animal muse—was going to help me do just that.

Additionally, Cathy promised to telepathically check on Jamie's welfare while in flight, to telepathically perform reiki on him to reduce stress and promote relaxation, and to telepathically hold my hand throughout the entire plane trip.

A few days before Mitzi would leave with her new person to live in Spain, she and Penny said goodbye to Jamie. At approximately 5:00 a.m., London Time, on August 21, 2012, a driver from the transportation company we hired picked up Jamie with all required flight documents, vaccination records, a "fit to fly" certificate, and his favorite toy taped to his travel-approved crate. The driver drove him to London's Heathrow Airport where he was booked on United Airlines Flight UA29, departing London at 10:05 a.m. and arriving in Newark, New Jersey, USA, at 1:00 p.m. Penny and I both anxiously waited for the transportation company's email confirming that one "live" Samoyed male weighing 24 kilograms was "handled with care" and safely enroute in a pressurized, climate-controlled cabin.

Last night at Penny's house

Last night at Penny's with his favorite toy
(Photos by Penny Roberts, used with permission)

Then it was Jamie's turn to leave the nest,
With his possessions taped to his crate,
Taken by car to Heathrow to wait.
As Penny and I forfeited rest
He must have heard the high-pitched cry
Of the massive birds spiraling high
As he was tethered behind a barrier
Safely in the cargo area.
Scared and alone in the darkness deep
I am sure he barked himself to sleep
As I waited in mild hysteria.

Penny and I, like shepherds keeping watch over their flocks, vigilantly tracked Jamie's flight; Cathy alternated between checking on Jamie and comforting me by relaying reports of his status; Hazel, his fans, and several of my friends held their collective breaths until he landed safely; and Ron drove me with haste, dodging rush hour traffic in three states to gather our traveler and bring him home.

Meanwhile, beginning to unravel,
Ron and I were anxious to travel.
With kibble, towels, water, and dish
We descended the driveway's gravel
Blowing to Corny a farewell kiss.
Then, we headed south, New Jersey bound.
We were lucky no traffic was found,
Until we crossed the river Hudson,
The Turnpike was under construction.
Keeping Exit 14 in our sight,
Looking for airplanes descending flight.
Following what the directions showed,
We took a left onto Brewster Road.
Looking for a space to park the car
Where we wouldn't have to walk too far.
Finally a spot on the rooftop.
We ran to Terminal C nonstop
Eager our new puppy to behold.

Ron and I arrived early at Newark and tried without any success to relax over a coffee. Shortly before one o'clock, we went to United Airline's PetSafe holding area to wait. With tears in my eyes, I introduced myself to the sympathetic attendant as an overly anxious owner of a Samoyed puppy arriving shortly on UA29. I must have presented myself as one unholy mess because as soon as the plane landed, she contacted the ground crew via cell phone as to the status of a white dog. Assured that he was fine, Ron and I were told to go outside, turn left, climb the stairs, and see for ourselves that the dogs would be the first passengers taken from the plane and loaded into a van. After approximately forty-five minutes, that van arrived at the holding area. There we could see but not touch him. Before we could do that, he needed to be seen by a veterinarian and clear Customs.

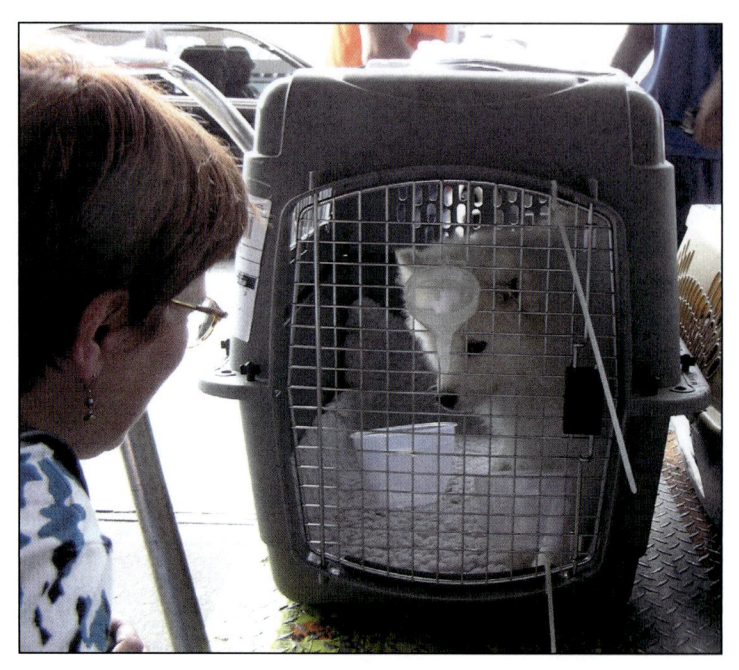

Jamie upon arrival at Newark, New Jersey
(Photo by Ron Reid, used with permission)

It was one by the concourse clock,
When he landed safely in Jersey town,
And was lifted onto the loading dock,
And into a van was quickly placed,
Feeling the wheels rumble as they raced,
Through the airport winding up and down.
Stopping, surely confused and afraid.
Who were those two strangers he beheld
As through glass doors he was conveyed
Looking at him with love unparalleled?

Finally, they released him into our care. I whispered a silent prayer of thanks to Penny as I noticed his favorite toy taped to the top of his crate. Our joint love for this darling puppy would link us forever. Hesitant, he allowed me to take him into my embrace. My arms, empty since April 7, 2010, were deliriously and finally full, and tears of happiness were watering those long thirsty tethering vines.

First embrace
(Photo by Ron Reid, used with permission)

When we arrived home, Ron stayed behind with Jamie as I ran inside to check on Corny. I brought her outside and stayed with her while Ron brought Jamie into the kitchen. To my amazement I noticed Jamie looking at us through our bedroom's French door. How did he know about the existence of that door, and how could he have known that it looked out onto our backyard? How could I love him without betraying Beau or Tristan? He knew, and I could because without me, Heaven wasn't home to Beau or Tristan. Did my heartache break the angels' hearts, and in sympathy did they return these souls to me? They had no choice; whatever our souls are made of, Beau's, Tristan's, Jamie's, and mine are the same, and wherever we are gathered, we are home.

So through the night flew our little boy;
And so through the morning I would text and post,
To friends overseas and coast to coast,
Words of anticipation and of joy
Which they would "share" immediately
With Facebook friends waiting impatiently
For news of the welfare of this cargo dear.
I know now there was nothing to fear
For the angels above had contrived
To answer by the wings of a bird
And ensuring the flight safely arrived
All the desires and wishes they heard.

And so ends my stolen Longfellow poem,
Of how a little British Pup found his way home.
Arriving here by land and by air
But his and my story doesn't end there.
To misquote the Patriot Paul Revere
More British are coming . . . here.

Jamie the Irresistible
(Photo by Beth Ortensi, used with permission)

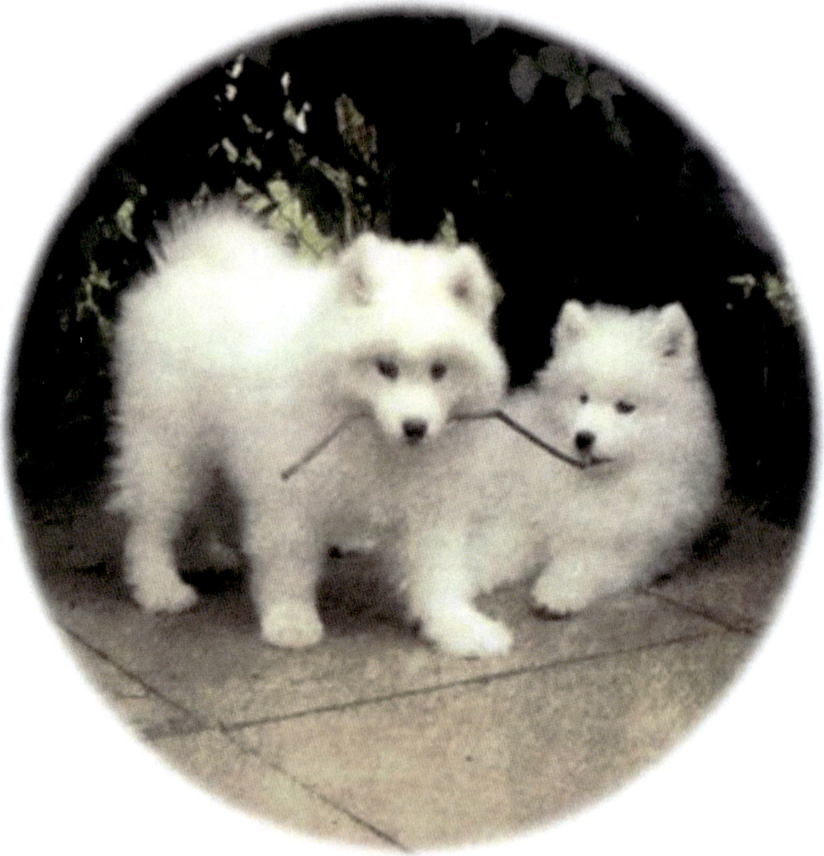

Geilie
My Angel of Pure Joy

(June 16, 2014–Present)

> Star light, star bright,
> The first star I see tonight;
> I wish I may, I wish I might,
> Have the wish I wish tonight.

She's a precious gemstone, in a little gift box wrapped in polka-dot paper and tied with a satin bow. She's tulle and whipped cream and snowflakes and pixie dust. She's pure joy and tickles. She's a whirling dervish, a spinning top, a ballerina pirouetting out of control. She's the brightest star in the sky. She's sunbeams, moonbeams, and lollipops. She's Coca Cola and chocolate cake. She's giggles and smiles and daffodils. She's Geillis and she's mine—all mine.

In July 2013, after I lost my beloved Corny, I found myself in a very dark place. My only consolation was my resolute belief in human and animal reincarnation. But would Corny return to me? Terribly insecure, I always felt that I could have done more to make her life more enjoyable. A sometimes "second-hand rose" to Tristan, my guilt was profound. Desperate to know if my beloved companion would return to me, I looked to Cathy Malkin and to Fiona Mauchlan, an intuitive coach, for answers. Both concurred that she would; however, Fiona prophetically added that not only would she return, but she would be the "life of the party and the belle of the ball."

Ron and I were now keen on Jamie's looks and personality and wanted, more than anything, for our next puppy to be of European stock. I contacted a breeder in Virginia who was planning a breeding with Jamie's uncle and waited for that breeding to occur.

For eleven months I looked to the Heavens and wished upon the stars with all my might, but I was looking south when I should have been looking northeast. Despite my insistence otherwise, Cathy was adamant that Geilie was hovering over Great Britain. You cannot imagine how astonished I was to read on Facebook that Penny and Hazel were each setting up whelping boxes as Flymo's sister, Abby, and Jamie's mother, Sunni, would soon each be whelping litters.

In mid-June 2014, ten Samoyed puppies, like pearls slipping off a string, fell from the sky. It was raining Samoyeds over Hertfordshire and Derbyshire, and Hazel and Penny honored me with the promise of a girl. Hallelujah. I wished I may and I wished I might, I got the wish I wished all those nights.

On June 14, 2014, Abby whelped seven puppies at Penny's house. On June 15, 2014, Cathy sensed that my Geilie would be born to Sunni. On June 16, 2014, Sunni whelped two boys and one girl, sired by Flymo's brother, Striker, at Hazel's house. These puppies were Jamie's half siblings.

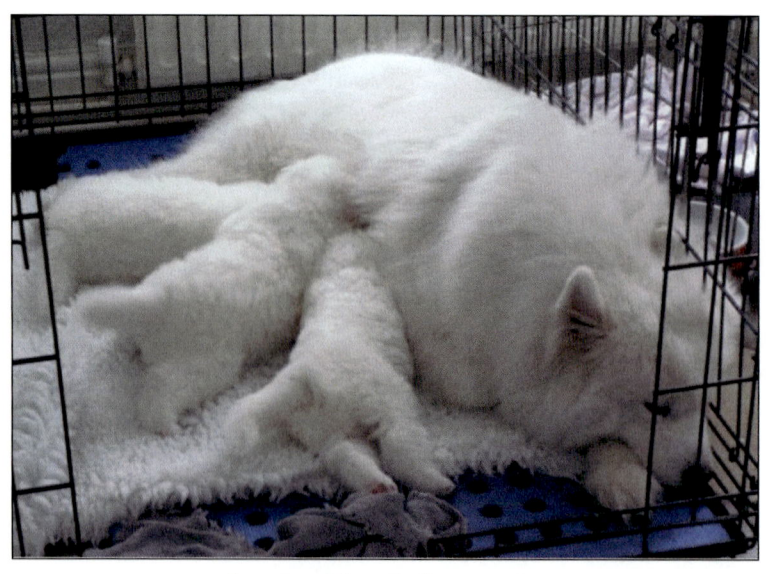

Sunni with her Striker puppies
(Photo by Hazel Fitzgibbon, used with permission)

I left it to Providence to decide which girl would be mine, but I did hope it would be Sunni's. Hazel didn't install a Puppy Cam over Sunni's whelping box, but she did share the dearest photos and videos of the puppies. Would the darling puppy with the cheeky smile and lovely biscuit-edged ears be mine? On July 22, 2014, Cathy's observation was realized, and we began preparing for her homecoming.

Smiliesam Striking Sunbeam—Puppy Geilie
(Photo by the author, Annie Reid)

Ice Maiden Smile Yoshi and us—Sunni
(Geilie's Dam)
(Photo from the private collection of Penny Roberts, used with permission)

Smiliesam Strike Home—Striker
Grand Champion of Slovakia, Champion UK
(Geilie's Sire and Jamie's Uncle)
(Photo by J.Kohvakka, used with permission)

*Puppy Geilie, handled with care by Matthew Arnold,
co-owner of Qi (Geilie's cousin and Jamie's half brother)
(Photo by Rachel Griffiths, used with permission)*

Because Penny's house is situated closer to Heathrow than Hazel's house is, it was arranged that Hazel would transport Geilie and return Sunni to Penny's the day before Geilie was to embark on her cross Atlantic trip. Penny and David enjoyed a day with Geilie, and Geilie spent a day with her father, Striker. On September 2, 2014, I—fortified with too much coffee and pumpkin spiced flavored donuts—settled in, with Penny keeping me company, for another long, sleepless summer night and stressful morning. When Ron and I finally arrived at Newark International Airport, a very excited, fearless, happy puppy exploded out of her crate like a firecracker, and she's been keeping us on our toes ever since.

*Geilie and me on the drive home from Newark Airport
(Selfie by the author, Annie Reid)*

My darling, silly Geilie
(Photo by the author, Annie Reid)

I named her after the "witch" in Diana Gabaldon's *Outlander* novels. Both her registered name, Smiliesam Striking Sunbeam, and her call name suit her to perfection. She is strikingly beautiful, charismatic, cheeky, and flashy, and I mistakenly thought these attributes would catapult her into American Kennel Club (AKC) stardom. Although she and Jamie are well within the published standard for the Samoyed breed, they are European-bred Samoyeds and, as such, appear smaller and too biscuit colored when standing alongside the American-bred Samoyeds. I refused a friend's suggestion to alter Geilie's appearance by applying powder to her lovely biscuit markings, and I wasn't keen on the idea of placing her in the care of a professional handler. With regrets, I eventually walked away from the AKC.

My dear friend Beth suggested I show Jamie and Geilie under the United Kennel Club (UKC) scheme. Beth is a fellow Samoyed owner, phenomenal photographer, and to my dismay, the other woman in Jamie's life. He adores her, and his adoration of this incredibly supportive, encouraging, and thoughtful woman is justified. Beth shows very successfully under both registries, but for six months out of the year we pitch tents and enjoy the more relaxed, but equally serious, UKC Conformation events.

Jamie, me, Geilie, and Beth Ortensi, August 12, 2017
(Photo by Katie Rogers, Smiling Wolf Photography, used with permission)

Jamie the Irresistible at a UKC event,
September 26, 2016
(Photo by Beth Ortensi,
used with permission)

My little sunbeam Geilie at a UKC event,
August 12, 2017
(Photo by the author,
Annie Reid)

The UKC promotes fair and amiable competition by prohibiting the use of professional handlers and by discouraging extreme grooming practices that would alter a dog's coat color or texture. Exhibitors may not groom or possess grooming tools within the ring and may not throw or litter the ring surface with bait. The judges often offer a short critique of their judging placements.

My irresistible Jamie at a UKC event, September 27, 2016
(Photo by Katie Rogers, Smiling Wolf Photography, used with permission)

My little sunbeam Geilie at a UKC event, September 26, 2015
(Photo by Katie Rogers, Smiling Wolf Photography, used with permission)

Both my spitfire Geilie and my more reserved Jamie have earned their UKC Champion titles as well as multiple Reserve Best in Show placements. Geilie has won one and Jamie has won two Best in Show placements.

Jamie, after winning Reserved Best in Show, August 9, 2015
(Photo by Katie Rogers, Smiling Wolf Photography, used with permission)

Geilie with her Reserve Best in Show rosettes
(Photo by the author, Annie Reid)

Jamie's championship photo
(Photo by Katie Rogers, Smiling Wolf Photography, used with permission)

My biscuit girlie Geilie, after winning Best in Show, September 10, 2017
(Photo by Katie Rogers, Smiling Wolf Photography, used with permission)

It is uncanny how much Jamie reminds me of Beau and Tristan. I look into his beautiful eyes and see the same reflection of love visible within. His favorite toy is Tristan's Frisbee. I love that he mashes his muzzle against my thigh whenever he wants my attention, that he is my sofa and bedmate, and that he is content just to be near me. Whenever he rests his head on my lap, I dissolve.

My irresistible Jamie
(Photo by the author, Annie Reid)

Geilie sleeps in Corny's favorite spot in the living room corner behind the piano whenever she is not engaging in thievery that would put Corny's abilities to shame. She is a very adept counter surfer.

My bewitching Geilie
(Photo by the author, Annie Reid)

But each dog has his or her own unique and charming personality. Jamie and Geilie are my treasures—my priceless gemstones. Jamie is like a pearl: he is innocence, beauty, purity, harmony, and dependability. Accordingly, life with Jamie is blissful, felicitous, and delightful. Jamie is perfection. Geilie is my opal: she is spontaneous, illuminating, energetic, fiery, mystical, bewitching, and exquisitely pleasing. Life with Geilie is unpredictable, exciting, and merry. Geilie is pure joy. Living with them is fairytale-like, and I hope nothing breaks this spell and wakes me from this most pleasant dream.

Geilie (Drawing by the author, Annie Reid, from a photograph by Katie Rogers, Smiling Wolf Photography)

Geilie and Jamie (Photo by the author, Annie Reid)

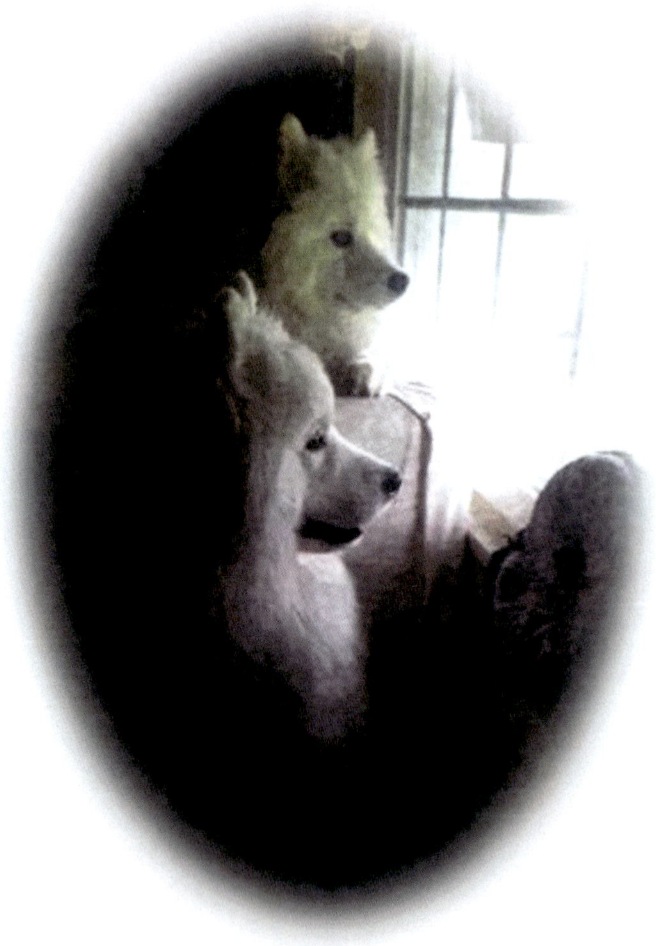

Tributes And Disclaimers

I chose "Macushla" as my kennel name. Macushla is the Anglicized form of "mo chuisle," a Gaelic term of endearment meaning "my darling, my sweetheart, my beloved." Niki, Beau, Corny, Tris, Jamie, and Geilie are my darlings, my sweethearts, my beloveds.

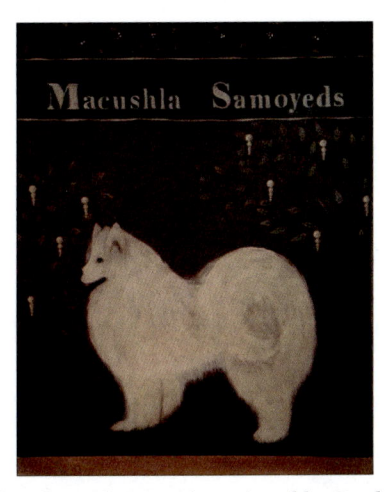

Wooden sign featuring Jamie, painted by Barbara Tautic
(Reprinted with the artist's permission)

I believe in and respect all creatures great and small. I believe in miracles and that with God all things are possible. I believe it takes many lifetimes for us to be deserving of Paradise and that God assigns each and every one of us guardians, or angels, to help us through each lifetime to eventually become gatherable wheat and not tares. I believe that many of these angels are our animal companions. I believe with all my heart that true love is indestructible and possesses energy strong enough to defy the bonds of death. I believe in the concept of soul mates.

Whatever my beliefs, I know one thing for certain: not everyone shares them. I find the phenomenon of animal communication and reincarnation comforting, but I want to make it very clear that with the exception of my animal communicators, the individuals mentioned in this narrative might consider such ideas ridiculous.

I think, however, we can agree that dogs enrich our lives. I am convinced that my dogs have influenced and continue to manipulate events that affect the quality of my life by introducing influential, caring, artistic, and spiritually healing people into my universe. If Beau had not accepted Ron, I would have been denied great joy, love, and happiness. I love and adore Ron with all my heart and cannot imagine life or lifetimes without him. If I didn't share Jim Cheskawich's mutual respect for the renowned Samoyed, Rex of White Way and hadn't bought several copies of his book *Rex of White Way, The Blizzard King*, we would not have collaborated on this Trilogy. When I was at my most vulnerable, my most disheartened, and my most inconsolable, Ron and Maura and Peggy and Barbara and Beth and Hazel and Penny and many other dear friends were there for me. And then there are all my animal communicators and my Samoyed Facebook friends with whom I share affection for this amazing breed; I love you all.

But, I am most grateful to Niki, Beau, Corny, Tristan, Jamie, and Geilie for choosing me. Jim, I can't thank you enough for giving me the opportunity to write my love story. As long as there is someone to read about mo chuisle, their spirits will never die.

Painting of Jamie and the inquisitive Geilie by Diane Buck and Barbara Tautic (Reprinted with each artist's permission)

Epilogue

When it was time to sell my childhood home, I didn't want the jewelry, the china, or the silver. I wanted the only item of value to me: my Niki's ashes. One fall evening at twilight I went into the backyard, found Niki's gravestone under her maple tree, and began to dig. The ground was hard and my twin, Maura, and her husband, Greg—seeing that I was crying and having difficulty—joined in the effort. This "gravely" solemn event turned comical when a nosey neighbor spotted us and notified the police. I guess our timing was bad. If you are going to rob a backyard grave, best not to do it during the "bewitching" hour.

We found my little girl where my father and I had buried her all those years ago, securely entombed in a tin box.

Maura sent her home with me in the one household item no one wanted: the clamshell shaped soup tureen. It seemed somewhat appropriate as that is where my mother always hid her valuables.

My most valuable family heirloom always had and always will have a place in my heart, but now Niki is home with me where she belongs.

Painting and floorcloth by Barbara Tautic
(Reprinted with the artist's permission)

Amen.

References and Sources

Brontë, Emily. *Wuthering Heights*. Franklin Square, New York: Harper & Brothers, 1858. https://archive.org/details/wutheringheight09brongoog.

Humperdinck, Engelbert. "Evening Prayer (When At Night I Go To Sleep)," *Hansel and Gretel*. New York, New York: Carl Fischer Music, 1893.

Shakespeare, William. *Romeo and Juliet*. New York: Sully and Kleinteich, c1901. http://etc.usf.edu/lit2go/201/romeo-and-juliet/4345/act-3-scene-2/.

Stevenson, Robert Louis. "Sing me a Song of a Lad that is Gone," *Songs of Travel*. London: Chatto & Windus, 1896.

Part III

Not Far From My Heart

By Cheryl Lynn West

Cheryl and Alicia at Fun Match.

Ditty, Alicia, and Quinder.

First in My Heart—Alicia

Lady Alicia of Wartland, CD, CGC

July 11, 1978 - August 28, 1991

Throughout our lives, we form bonds with others—our parents, sisters and brothers, friends, and yes, our spouses. But these bonds are not limited to humans. We refer to our canine companions as our heart dogs and talk about our undying love for them. Those who have not experienced this may scoff and tell us "it's only a dog;" they may think that we are projecting our feelings onto an animal. I can tell you that these people are so wrong. There is a binding connection that time and distance cannot break.

I need to back up to explain my story, so please bear with me. I had pets when growing up, but these never stayed long. My first pet, an unnamed cat, was a stray that didn't even make it a whole day. I was five and convinced my mother and father to let me bring a large tabby into the house. Like most, we believed in the adage that cats like milk. A large consumption of milk led to an abrupt case of diarrhea and an immediate ouster of the cat.

My next pet was a dog named Trixie. She came to live with us when we moved to Sunset Valley in Irwin, Pennsylvania. This was one of those new housing developments, exploding across America as the soldiers back from World War II were moving their families from the city to a suburban setting. I was six years old and along with my mother and father, Helen and Chuck Duncan, my eleven-year-old sister Bonnie, and my two-year-old sister Denise, moved into our first home. This American dream included having a dog, a cute puppy we named Trixie. However, my parents were of the generation that believed dogs belonged outside when we weren't home. They tied Trixie to the outside stairs that rose from the basement up one floor to the kitchen door, as the house was on a slope. The steps were open risers, and Trixie must have tried to climb to the kitchen door. I was the one to find her, already gone, hanging from her leash and collar. To this day, tears come to my eyes when I think about Trixie. How do you explain to a child that her puppy is gone? Other pets—Pudgie, Lady, Zorro, Midnight—followed through the years. I would love them dearly, but each would disappear, with the dogs given away and the cats going for midnight runs.

My family had moved back to Swissvale, a small suburb just on the outskirts of Pittsburgh. Our home was a duplex with a backyard the size of a postage stamp. Neighbors were close in all senses of the word. Ann McGough, our elderly maiden landlady, lived in the other half of the duplex. Although she shared her house with a sweet, shaggy mutt, her tenants were not permitted to have dogs. It seemed that my pets would be limited to the stuffed variety. That changed briefly when a purebred Irish Setter entered my life.

The Walt Disney Productions movie, *Big Red,* was the summer hit in 1962. My father would drive me to the Regent Square Theater where I would stay for both showings of the Saturday matinee, munching on fresh theater popcorn between tears for Rene and Big Red. Just like every boy and girl throughout America, I fell in love with Big Red. A local after-school TV show, *Captain Jim's Popeye Club,* was having a contest in which all one had to do was send in a postcard; the winner would become the owner of the most beautiful creature on earth. I begged my parents to let me enter. *"Please, I would take care of the dog and just love him so much,"* forgetting about the no-dogs rule. Mom and Dad looked at each other, telling me it was okay to send in a postcard. After all, what chance did I have of winning? You guessed it. On June 27, Captain Jim reached into that rotating barrel of tumbling postcards, and out came my postcard. I had the winning entry, and I wasn't even watching the show! After the show went off the air, we got a phone call from the WIIC-TV station, telling me that I was the lucky winner, and they wanted to bring "my" Big Red to me the very next day. I was barely off the phone when our landlady was knocking on our front door. We were NOT allowed to keep the dog. Another neighbor had been watching the show with her children and had immediately let her know about "the dog." A young, adorable, and rambunctious Irish Setter bounded throughout our house the next afternoon. I can still remember Red (what else would I call him) putting his front feet on my four-foot, ten-inch tall grandmother, slobbering her face with kisses. Unfortunately, we had no choice, and Red went to a new family who had a farm. I had just twenty-four hours of love with him. And while I was unable to keep Red, we did have another addition to our family. My youngest sister Maureen was born on June 30. Being a typical sister, I told her many times as we grew up that I wished we had kept the dog instead. We laugh now as Maureen shares my love for dogs and would probably say the same.

So much for my childhood and pets. I share this so that you can understand my pledge that any pet I would have, once I was an adult, would never leave me except through death. I would not be a person to discard a beloved canine or feline for any reason. And so far, I have kept that promise with one exception, one that broke my heart although I knew it was "for the best." I so hate that phrase.

This is the story of Alicia, my first Samoyed. My husband at the time, Ken Wisniewski, promised that when we bought our first house, I could have a dog. We had four cats already, all rescues—Rusty, K.C., Solomon and Fritz. I have loved all my cats through the years, and we are still a "mixed" family—cats and dogs together. But I really wanted a dog and was very specific about what that dog should be—four legs, two ears and one tail—any of those negotiable. I just wanted a dog. We borrowed books from the library and researched so many different breeds. We finally decided that the perfect dog would be a Golden Retriever. Next came the job of finding our puppy, which quickly became a problem. We had no idea how to find someone who bred pedigreed dogs other than searching the classified ads in the Sunday paper. Remember this was back in 1978. Unbelievably, there were no Golden Retrievers listed. I began to lose hope of getting my puppy.

Fate took an interesting twist that summer. Ken was driving through North Park near Pittsburgh when he saw a woman walking a beautiful furry white dog. He practically drove the car off the road, stopped, jumped out of the car, and ran towards the woman, yelling "What is that dog?" I guess she must have been used to this reaction as she yelled back, "A Samoyed." Fast forward to my birthday on August 7. As he usually did something special for it, I was not surprised when he called me at work and said he was taking me somewhere special. I figured maybe dinner at a quaint restaurant. We drove out into the country. This wasn't the route to one of our favorite places, and he wouldn't give me even the slightest clue. Ken turned into the driveway, and a couple came out to greet us. "You're here to see about the puppies." I could not believe my ears. A PUPPY! I didn't even know what breed they were but I was there to pick out my very own puppy.

Cheryl holding Alicia, October 1978.

The couple led us into the garage at the back of the house. In the whelping box was "Spot," a Samoyed bitch with her litter of five-week-old puppies. Wait a minute. Isn't this an all-white dog? The husband laughed and said her actual name was the Duchess Dehaven. However, as a child, he had loved the *Dick and Jane* stories and had always wanted a dog just like Spot. We played with the puppies and finally selected one of the girls. I had to wait three long weeks until the puppies were old enough to leave their mother. So, on Labor Day we drove back, and Alicia became our first dog, officially and regally named Lady Alicia of Wartland. At times, she had a few other names, such as Berserko Puppy for all the trouble she managed to create. But she was always a delightful and energetic ball of fluff.

Alicia drew me into the life of a dog owner, not just as a pet but all the way to

Alicia winning Best Adult at Greater Pittsburgh Samoyed Fanciers' match.

Conformation, Obedience, breeding, sled racing, weight pulling, sheep herding, therapy, dog clubs, and of course, like-minded dog owners. And as anyone knows, that is another whole class of people. Life also threw in a myriad of changes, including a move from Pittsburgh, Pennsylvania, to Winter Springs, Florida. Some of these changes were good; others were not so good. We expanded our canine family with Alicia's son, Quinder, before leaving Pittsburgh and brought Ditty, a friend's Samoyed, into our house and our hearts in Florida. During this time, my marriage fell apart. The tense situation affected the dogs, pitting Alicia and Ditty against each other. The term "bitch fight" was the appropriate phrase. The battles were furious, with multiple puncture wounds on both dogs and even resulting a broken leg for Alicia during one of the fights. It reached the point that I had to make the painful decision of giving up one of the girls, a truly Solomonic choice. Ken was now my ex-husband, but he did love the dogs as I did. Did I send Alicia to him, breaking the promise never to part with one of my animals, or did I send Ditty, who had already been bounced from her first home? Ditty had a fear of men; in fact, it had taken over six months before she would accept Ken's touch. I would have rather been cut in half than make the choice. In the end, it came down to Ken taking Alicia with the promise that I would get her back at his death. He had kidney and liver cancer and only a short time to live.

Ken died about a year later, and Alicia was to come back to me. However, that would have given me the problem of two bitches in one house when each had been top dog in separate homes. And Alicia was almost twelve years old. My good friend, Betty Dunlevy, agreed to take Alicia into her home in Pittsburgh, and I could see her when I visited. My heart broke again as I stood in the airport terminal, watching my beautiful girl being loaded onto the plane. Tears flow again as I write this. I had broken my promise not once but twice, and Alicia was leaving again.

Paul and Betty gave Alicia the best home, one filled with love and a caring touch. We talked often, and Betty raved about Alicia's sweetness and at times, her little quirks. The strangest one was the worn, orange, squeaky ball which accompanied Alicia on her trip north. The ball was the last of Alicia's "puppies" from her false pregnancies. After Alicia's first and only litter, we kept her intact so that we could show her. Following each subsequent heat cycle until she was spayed, Alicia exhibited visible signs of pregnancy and on the sixtieth day produced a litter of "puppies" consisting of all her rubber toys. There was Green Frog Boy, Little Yellow Ball Girl, Blue Bone Boy and of course, Large Orange Ball Girl. She would press them to her stomach for nursing, clean them incessantly and even be reluctant to leave them unless I would watch over them. Betty chuckled, recounting how Alicia

Alicia, feeding six of her ten puppies, born March 23, 1980.

would cuddle daily with the orange ball, licking and squeaking it for what seemed hours. Betty was too kindhearted to even think of taking Alicia's toy away although she did look for ear plugs several times.

Time went on, and I married Frank, a wonderful man and the love of my life. Alicia had gone to live with Betty about a year earlier, and Frank and I had been married about a month. It was a ten o'clock on a Sunday night in August, and we were preparing for bed. Frank bent over to kiss me, and I burst into tears. Just what a newly married man wants—his wife crying hysterically in bed. He was distressed and wanted to know what was wrong. "Alicia is going to die," I sobbed. Holding me gently, he replied, "Yes," as Alicia was old. "No, Alicia is going to die—soon!" I cried myself to sleep that night.

The next day, I met up with friends after work for dinner, returning home at about eight o'clock. Betty had phoned and wanted me to call back. "Is Alicia dead?" I asked. Frank shook his head as Betty had not left any further message.

My hands shaking, I dialed Betty. When she answered, I immediately asked, "Is Alicia dead?" "Yes," Betty softly answered. They had taken her into the veterinarian that morning to release her from her suffering. I had to know: When had they made that decision? Betty replied that Alicia had taken a very bad turn at ten o'clock the night before, and they knew it was time to say goodbye.

Even though I could not be there, Alicia and I were together at that moment. To this day I feel that her spirit came to say goodbye to me—one last time—and sent her love. I still hold my beautiful girl in my heart, and she will always be part of me. And I am thankful that Betty and Paul Dunlevy gave Alicia their hearts also.

Alicia, Winter Springs, Florida.

Alicia, resting after a day of hiking.

ALICIA

I have to say goodbye now.
I can't stay any longer.
But I wanted to stop and say
Thank you all so very much.

You gave me a home
And a bed next to yours.
You gave me treats.
I always wanted more.

You gave me pats on the head
And loads of huge bear hugs.
You gave me long brushings.
You could have skipped the baths.

Most of all, you gave me your love,
Every single day and more.
Even that last day, with tears,
You gave me the gift of peace.

So now I'm on my way,
To play forever more.
I'll run and bark and laugh
And stop to smile at you.

I just wanted you to know
That when you gave me your heart,
I lovingly gave you mine,
Right from the very start.

Cheryl, her nephew and Ditty.

Ditty and Alicia, Christmas 1985.

A New Friend–Ditty

Baresof's Sheeza Pepper, CD

May 15, 1982 - July 3, 1997

A friend asked on Facebook if anyone had ever seen a ghost. He was shocked and intrigued when I answered "yes." Only it wasn't a ghostly human spirit nor a vague form of plasma and light. It was that of my Itty Bitty Ditty, a sweet Samoyed girl who had a way of working herself into your heart. Her registered name was Baresof's Sheeza Pepper. My friend, Ditty's original owner and breeder, tried various call names, such as Sheeza, but this little girl refused to acknowledge them. It wasn't until my friend commented on the little girl's size, joking, "She's such an itty bitty ditty" that the puppy's ears perked up. Ditty had selected her own name.

Ditty joined our family in Florida in 1982 after my friend had to walk away from her marriage. This meant giving up her Samoyeds as she was unable to take all but one with her. She asked if I wanted Ditty as a playmate with my Alicia and her puppy Quinder. Once Ditty came to live with us, though, it became apparent that there had been other unknown problems. Ditty had an extreme fear of men. If she felt threatened by a man and was unable to get away, she would go into a "freeze mode"—Ditty's eyes would glaze over, her stance became rigid, and she turned into a furry, white, unmoving statue. She also had hot spots and was badly stained from chewing herself, another sign of stress. The Ditty I had known, when I lived in Pittsburgh, was a sweet, outgoing puppy who loved to show and sparkle. With time and love, Ditty did regain much of her personality as she didn't fear women. It did take great effort, especially as any man seemed like a monster to her. This poem, written while Ditty was alive, shows how she blossomed again into the essence of what a Samoyed is.

The question is—What is a Ditty?
The answer easy—A small Sammy bitch.
But now just try to describe her.
Oh, yes, here comes the glitch.

With a compact body and high-pitched voice,
She's a screwball, a furry-faced clown.
Whether stealing a bone or cuddling close,
Ditty does all things with nary a frown.

Wearing discarded clothes and fancy beads,
She patiently sits while being dressed up.
Flash dancer, cowboy, even an old grandmother,
We turn her into a high fashion pup.

Ditty loves the water behind our house
And leaps after sticks and quacking ducks.
She fetches the sticks to be thrown again.
With ducks, thank goodness, she has no luck.

Carrying sprinklers, beer cans, and neighbors' balls,
She cleans my yard with its weed and sand.
When she brought a dead squirrel, torn in half,
I felt this trick had gotten out of hand.

She hops after frogs, crickets, and lizards,
Stomping my flowers down to the ground.
She picks the tomatoes off the vine
And gobbles them up when no one is around.

She holds the record for most baths in a day.
Keeping her clean is a full-time chore.
The neighbors have horses, both large and small,
Is there really a need to say more?

A guard, she sleeps by my bed at night.
In the morning, she eats her food like a hog.
She's my buddy, always a joy to behold.
Ditty is just—simply my dog.

Ditty, swimming in Lake Wanter, another reason for her need of frequent baths.

My friend had updated Ditty's shots before sending her to Florida to be with me. As Ditty was just turning two years old, she had decided to have Ditty's hips x-rayed and learned that Ditty was dysplastic. She asked if I wanted to change my mind. No, I was committed to taking Ditty. Dysplasia is a genetic, ongoing condition, and each dog reacts to it differently. Ditty's was severe. If she stressed herself from exertion and hurt herself, she would again turn into a "pillar of salt" as the pain made the slightest movement intolerable. She didn't cry or bite as some dogs might have done. However, with the kind care of our veterinarian, Dr. Alex Suero, we were able to give Ditty relief and a good quality of life. There were many more good days than bad ones. We even managed to get a Novice Obedience title on her. But as anyone who has Samoyeds knows, it is never an easy process. It may be interesting, challenging, and delightful to ringside observers but never easy.

While Ditty improved, my personal life disintegrated, resulting in a divorce from my first husband. After we separated and he moved out of the house, there was no leader of the pack. The fighting between Ditty and Alicia reached a point that I had to place one and keep the other. Given Ditty's background, I made the difficult decision that she needed to stay with me. I think for some time I resented that, but there is no way that one can ever stay mad at a beloved pet, especially a Samoyed like Ditty.

Eventually, I managed to get my act together, and Ditty, Quinder, and I—along with the cats—moved forward. Frank joined us in 1991, and Ditty fell in love with him. It is a testimony to Frank's nature that a dog who was terrified of men instantly and

Ditty and Cheryl, Seminole Dog Fancier's Association Halloween party, 1985.

totally adored him. Life went on, and other Samoyeds, Sultan and Luke, became part of the Castle Samoyed clan. Ditty was the only female, the sole queen among her lowly male subjects. Oh, and did she rule with an iron paw. She may have batted her eyes, but get too close and she would send any boy flying. Laura Segers, the breeder of Sultan and Luke, didn't believe me until one day when she was visiting with her Sabre. This gorgeous male Samoyed was enamored with Ditty. She daintily sashayed into her crate, giving him that inviting look. Sabre followed, tail wagging, only to suddenly and swiftly moonwalk backwards from her abode.

While ever feisty, time and the dysplasia took their tolls. There came the day of that final decision, the one we all dread. Frank was on a motorcycle trip, and I made the last drive with Ditty alone. We later buried Ditty in the backyard to rest with Quinder under the cherrybark oak tree.

Time passed, and we added Skye and Deirdre to our pack. But Alicia, Quinder, and Ditty were never far from my heart. Several years later, just as the dawn was breaking, I awoke and gazed out the bedroom window towards the cherrybark oak tree. There, in the shimmering mist, I saw a white shape. It grew more distinct, and I saw it was Ditty. My heart leaped for joy, and I called out in my mind, "Ditty, come here." My sweet girl started towards the house. I felt the tears rising in my eyes. Then she stopped and turned her head back. I saw another Samoyed, a female standing hesitantly in the fog. Ditty looked again at me, a wistful expression in her eyes. I heard her words, "I can't come. I have a new friend to take care of." Ditty returned to her friend, and the two disappeared into the mist. My heart broke again, but I knew my Ditty was needed elsewhere.

I went back to sleep but not for long. Not wanting to disturbing Frank, I went to the family room at the front of the house and as was the norm, logged onto the internet. There I read a message from Mary Carlson, a fellow Samoyed owner who lived in Arizona. She had written to a group list that she had lost her girl, Moon-Fire's Ideal Margarita, during the night. I responded, letting her know that Margee was okay, and Ditty was with her. It gave both of us peace to share this knowledge.

Some may say it was a dream, but I know better. I did see a ghost. Ditty, that sweet little Sammy bitch, returned this one time to let me know she would always be in my life.

Itty Bitty Ditty.

Ditty in the woods.

My Sweet Baby Boy–Duncan

Int. CH. White Gold's Highlander of the Castle, HT, PT, HCT-s, JHD-s

May 3, 2009 - August 2, 2016

Duncan

Each of our canine companions is a special, unique being. Perhaps this is one of the reasons we can keep them in our hearts, separate but equal, memories so clear that we feel we are talking about just yesterday when we recount our lives with them. It is that way with Duncan, partially because he died only last year. And the pain is heightened as he is my only Samoyed who died at a young age. I have been blessed, if that is the word, over the thirty-five plus years of owning Samoyeds that my dogs have lived long lives. In a sense, whether their departure was due to age or a long-term disease such as cancer, Frank and I had the time to prepare ourselves and to say goodbye, even in a flood of tears.

Before I tell you about the last day with Duncan and his second farewell, I so much want to share some tales of Duncan's life. Duncan was named after my father, Charles Paul Duncan. My father lived his entire life in Pittsburgh, other than his service in Germany during World War II. Like most men of that era, Dad never spoke about the things he had seen or done, except for his misadventures during leave in Paris. His jokes were lighthearted with a bit of teasing of my four sisters and me. There were so many dinners with bantering going back and forth, each trying to top the other. But no one could outdo my father. He had a slight tilt of his head and a smile that made you suspect he wasn't quite telling the truth, but he spoke with such sincerity at the same time. He shared my love of the dogs and encouraged me to enter the show ring. I had grown up an extremely shy girl, often fainting in class when I had to give a speech. Dad saw my confidence when I was in the ring with Alicia and Quinder, my first two Samoyeds.

My dad always joked that he wanted to return as one of my dogs when he died as I treated them so well. I reminded him that I get all my male dogs neutered once they are done being shown. Dad laughed and said he had changed his mind. He loved his five daughters with all his soul, and his sudden death hit us hard. I had spoken my last words to him the week before when he waited as I boarded the plane back to Florida. I had turned around and yelled, "I love you, Dad."

Twenty-five years after my father's death, Duncan, the puppy, came into our lives. He was given the regal name of White Gold's Highlander of the Castle. While he didn't care for the show ring, earning the name "Punkie Dunkie," he loved herding sheep. Maybe Duncan had Highlander blood in him. Sheep herding took thought, and Duncan loved to be the one to decide how and where the sheep would be moved. His biggest frustration was with me as I was the dummy in the field. If I didn't move fast enough or where he wanted the sheep to be, he had no problem in vocally scolding me.

We were working on Barn Hunting, a sport in which a domestic rat is placed in a capped PVC tube with plenty of air holes. Three tubes—one empty, one with soiled

Duncan, three months old.

straw, and the third with the rat—are hidden in stacked hay bales. The object is for the dog to find the tube with the rat. It was amazing to see Duncan quickly realize the goal of this event. Once we entered the enclosure, Duncan sat and began to sniff the air, slowly turning his head in each direction. With me encouraging him, he went from bale to bale, poking his head in the bales and pawing at the loose hay. Suddenly, he dove straight into the crevice between two bales, only his tail showing. I screamed "Rat," letting the judge know that Duncan had indeed found the correct tube!

Duncan at his first Barn Hunting competition.

But it was with people that Duncan excelled. Like my father, there was never a person who did not like Duncan. Nor was there a person whom Duncan did not love. Even more amazing was the way Duncan would cock his head, tilted off to the side with an ever-present smile. That was my dad as well, head tilted and smiling. Yes, Duncan did remind me of my father.

Duncan had a knack for getting his way. He loved to be outside in the yard under his "leave me be tree." Loxley and Gwen, my two younger Samoyeds, would run around the yard until it was too hot in the Florida heat, then rush to come inside to the cool air conditioning. Duncan didn't mind the heat. He would sit in the back of the yard, facing away from the house like a sentry on guard duty. If I didn't let the dogs outside, Duncan would take matters into his own "paws." Putting his snout between the wall and handle of the sliding glass door, he would push the door open, just enough to squeeze through. Loxley and Gwen quickly followed. The solution to this "Great Escape" was simple—just move the latch into the locked position, a tactic that worked just one day. Duncan, like most Samoyeds, was a thinker and must have watched me pushing the latch down to unlock it. Taking that knowledge, Duncan pawed the door, his toenail catching the latch. Click, the door was unlocked, and Duncan once again was soon on the other side. In case I thought this was a fluke, he did this each time I locked the door until it became necessary to put a piece of PVC piping in the door track.

I was not the only one to be outwitted by Duncan. The two boys were best buds, closer than any other male dogs I have seen. Loxley was two years younger than Duncan, and as a puppy, he would latch onto Duncan's tail and be pulled across the grass. Loxley eventually outweighed Duncan by ten pounds, and avoiding Loxley's tail-yanking grip became a daily challenge for Duncan. Attempting to get the advantage, Loxley would bolt out the door and stand in front of the large yucca plant. He beamed in anticipation, just waiting for Duncan to venture off the screened porch. When Loxley was successful in leaping on Duncan, the "bromance" would turn into a rough and tumble wrestling match with the boys knocking each other into the dirt, then racing around the yard. Of course, Duncan—being the brains in the duo—knew exactly what was going to happen. Duncan stood in the open doorway, beaming back. Loxley would hide behind the plant, but he was still in sight as the plant offered little cover. Duncan wouldn't budge. At this point, Loxley would lie down, peeking through the leaves, making himself as low as possible. "Loxley, Duncan can still see you." Duncan shifted his weight to the left, and Loxley committed. Duncan quickly leaped to the right in a burst of speed. Off he raced, Loxley chasing far behind across the yard. Score, Duncan—again.

Loxley attempting to hide from Duncan.

In August 2016 Duncan was just a little over seven years old. It was a typical Florida summer day with the dogs going outside only briefly. Looking back, I try to see signs that Duncan was in distress, but they either weren't there or were easily mistaken as being minor. When Duncan refused to eat his dinner, I knew something wasn't right. I grabbed Duncan's head and saw that his gums were white. Frank and I raced Duncan to the veterinarian's office, only ten minutes away. Duncan was in total collapse as we rushed him inside. We made it only to lose Duncan within minutes of our arrival. Nothing prepared us for this, and the veterinarian was unable to say what had happened. It was only later that we learned that Duncan had bloated, showing none of the usual signs.

Grief consumed me and devastated both Frank and me. I missed so many things about Duncan. Even the start of the day had been dependent on Duncan's whims. Gwen slept between Frank and me, but Duncan was the one who had determined when we arose. He would push Gwen aside and lie next to me. If I ignored him, he would flop himself across my face and chest. Now, we are talking a fifty-five pound, extremely furry dog. If I managed to continue to breathe, Duncan would get off the bed and ram my ribs full force with his nose. There was no denying that final wake-up call. The day had officially begun.

Adding to our grief was the knowledge that Rasia, our fourteen-year-old Samoyed, was in failing health. Age was taking its toll, and it was obvious that we would soon be saying goodbye. Ten days after Duncan's death, I was lying in bed, Gwen and Loxley were in the bathroom on the cool tile floor, and Rasia was sleeping outside the bathroom. I listened to the rise and fall of Rasia's slow, raspy breathing. Suddenly, without warning, I was rammed in the ribs, hard and swift. I whirled, expecting to see Duncan, but no one was there. Yet I knew it was him. Later that day, at lunchtime, we let the two younger dogs outside for a break. As Rasia stood to follow them, she could not support herself. Prior to this, Rasia had needed some assistance to stand, but once on her feet, she was able to walk. On this day her back feet turned under, having lost mobility in her rear. We knew it was time to say goodbye. And we knew that Duncan had come earlier to help her cross the Rainbow Bridge.

That was not our only visit with Duncan. The day after Duncan's death, Loxley had raced outside and waited for Duncan to come play the hiding game behind the yucca plant. He stood in front of the plant, moved behind, and finally laid down. I burst into tears. Loxley waited, then walked off into the yard. Loxley was missing his buddy, just as we were. He seemed to adapt quickly and did not look for Duncan after that—except for one last time. A day after Rasia's death, Loxley went into the yard and stood in front of the yucca plant again. But this time was different. He had a focused look that was riveted on the porch screen door. I called to him, but he showed no recognition of my voice. Instead, Loxley moved behind the plant and lay down, locking his stare on the door. I called again, moving, trying to divert his eyes. He was seeing something that I could not see, and he would not break off. We stood that way for another minute or two, then there was a change in Loxley's posture. He relaxed and turned, going lightly into the backyard. I did not see him, but I knew with my full being that Duncan had been there. Loxley had played their game one last time.

In closing, I want to share one last story, one that is not about Duncan. For two long years in high school, I tried to learn French. One story we read was about a mother who had lost her young son. She prayed to God to give her son back to her, and God made this promise: she was to visit the homes in her village, and if she could find just one family who had not lost someone, her son would be returned to her. Journeying street by street, she found that each family had lost someone dear to them. Because her fellow villagers had also suffered deeply, they were able to comfort her, helping her deal with her grief. Such was the outpouring of love from my family and friends throughout the dog community after the deaths of our dogs. Part of loving our pets is knowing that we will lose them much too soon and sometimes without warning. It is heartrending at times. I am thankful for the loving and continual support and comfort from these friends. For this, I am truly grateful.

Duncan in backyard, March 2016.

About the Authors

Jim Cheskawich is an award winning author with gold and silver global eLit and eBook awards for *The Story of Rex of White Way-The Blizzard King*. The book also won the Maxwell Award from the Dog Writers' Association of America for the best single breed book in 2013. He founded and was the first president of the Rex of White Way Samoyed Memorial Library and Museum. His second book, *Vietnam 1971: Remembering the "101st" Then and Now* won two gold medals in a global eBook competition for Best Autobiography/Memoir and Best in Military. He substitute teaches in several school districts in the Battle Ground, WA area, serves as a volunteer assistant football coach at La Center High School, manages a boarding kennel, and is the Senior Vice Commander and Canteen Manager for the Gus Forbes Woodland VFW Post 1927. He retired in 2002 as the HR Director for Mine Safety and Health Administration, U.S. Department of Labor. He has a B.S. in Management and MBA from Penn State University and has been past president and treasurer and is a current board member for the Samoyed Club of America.

Growing up, **Annie Reid** had two passions—drawing and her Samoyed, Niki. The Samoyed has always been Annie's favorite subject and her award winning drawings of them suggest very close and warm relationships with her Samoyeds as well as a genuine admiration and respect for the breed. Now she is using words as an element of expression to deliver a message of love triumphant. Annie and her husband, Ron, live in Connecticut in blissful harmony with their Samoyeds, Jamie and Geilie. She is proud of Jamie's and Geilie's international bloodlines and equally proud of her Irish, English and Scottish pedigree (she is a descendant of Mary Queen of Scots).

Cheryl Lynn West has long enjoyed both the technical and literary worlds. She graduated from Carnegie Mellon University with a double degree in Chemical Engineering and English Literature. Her business career included Naval Nuclear Project Management for Westinghouse Electric Corporation and Quality Engineering and Auditing at Siemens Power Generation Division. Prior to retirement, Cheryl became Editor-in-Chief of the Samoyed Club of America, Inc. Bulletin. She lives with her husband, Frank, in Casselberry, Florida, and stays busy, focusing on her creative pursuits of writing, photography, graphic design and painting. These pursuits are only surpassed by her long love of Samoyeds, and the many facets of the dog world.

Made in the USA
Middletown, DE
11 August 2019